PURSUIT TO APPOMATTOX
The Last Battles

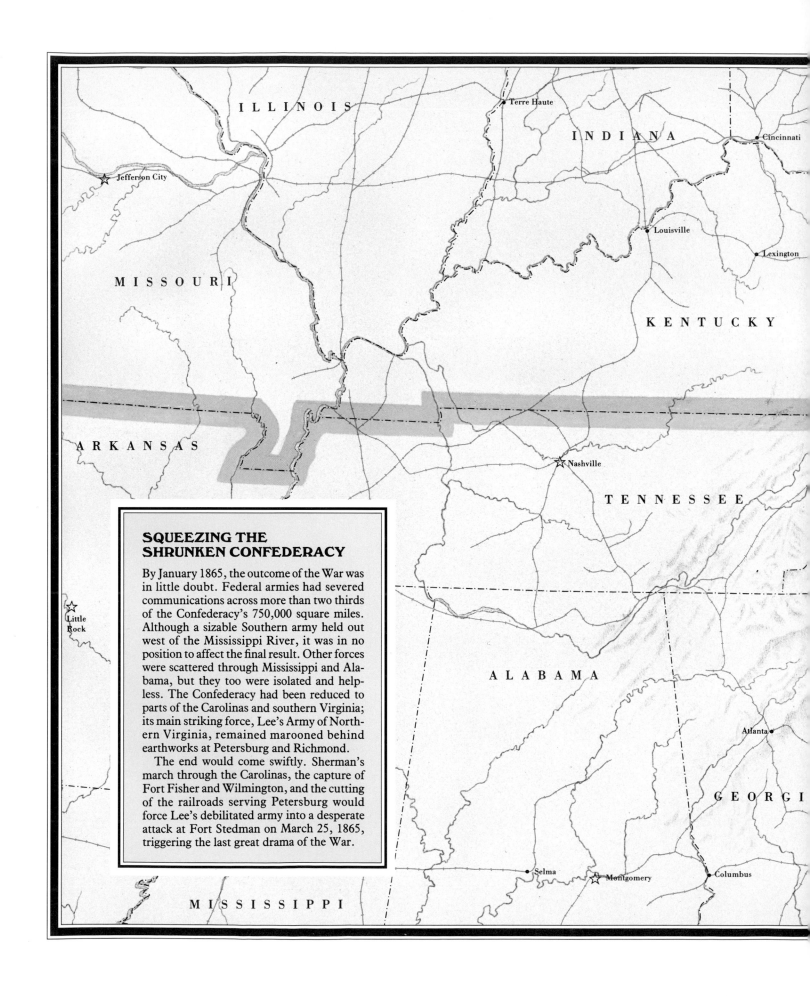

ILLINOIS

INDIANA

• Terre Haute

• Cincinnati

☆ Jefferson City

• Louisville

• Lexington

MISSOURI

KENTUCKY

ARKANSAS

☆ Nashville

TENNESSEE

☆
Little
Rock

SQUEEZING THE SHRUNKEN CONFEDERACY

By January 1865, the outcome of the War was in little doubt. Federal armies had severed communications across more than two thirds of the Confederacy's 750,000 square miles. Although a sizable Southern army held out west of the Mississippi River, it was in no position to affect the final result. Other forces were scattered through Mississippi and Alabama, but they too were isolated and helpless. The Confederacy had been reduced to parts of the Carolinas and southern Virginia; its main striking force, Lee's Army of Northern Virginia, remained marooned behind earthworks at Petersburg and Richmond.

The end would come swiftly. Sherman's march through the Carolinas, the capture of Fort Fisher and Wilmington, and the cutting of the railroads serving Petersburg would force Lee's debilitated army into a desperate attack at Fort Stedman on March 25, 1865, triggering the last great drama of the War.

ALABAMA

Atlanta •

GEORGI

• Selma

☆ Montgomery

• Columbus

MISSISSIPPI

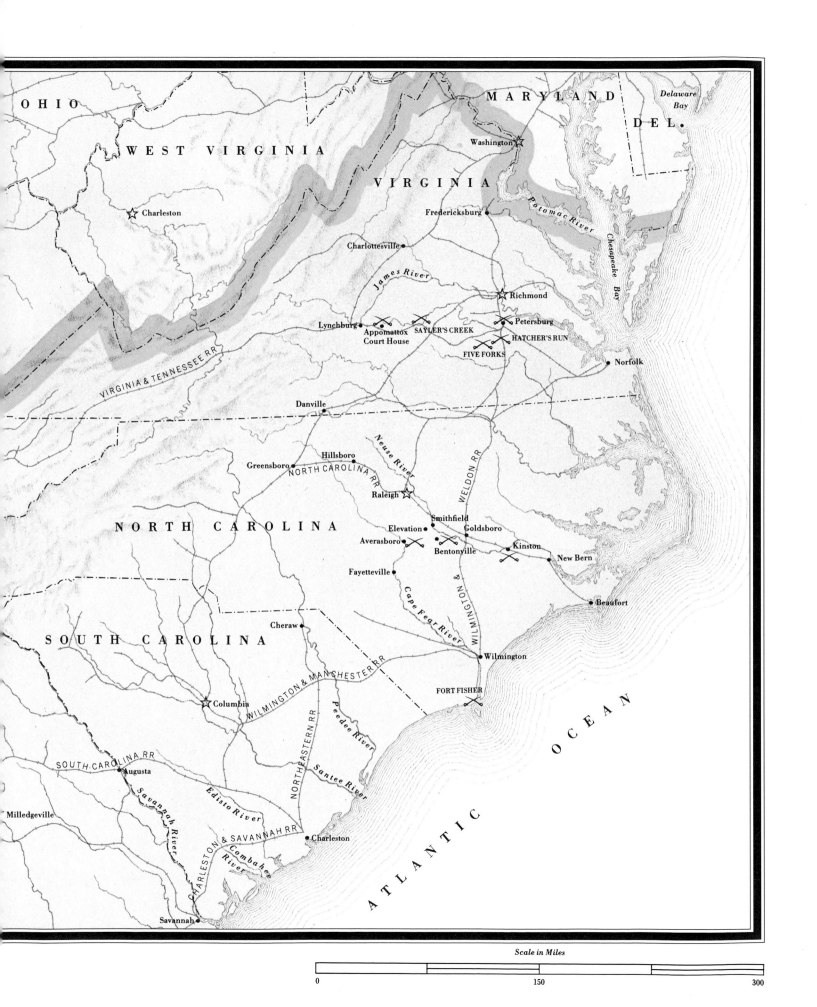

OHIO

WEST VIRGINIA

MARYLAND

DEL.

Delaware Bay

VIRGINIA

Washington

Potomac River

Charleston

Fredericksburg

Charlottesville

Chesapeake Bay

James River

Richmond

Lynchburg

Appomattox Court House

SAYLER'S CREEK

Petersburg

HATCHER'S RUN

FIVE FORKS

Norfolk

VIRGINIA & TENNESSEE RR

Danville

Hillsboro

Greensboro

Neuse River

NORTH CAROLINA RR

WELDON RR

Raleigh

NORTH CAROLINA

Elevation

Smithfield

Goldsboro

Averasboro

Bentonville

Kinston

New Bern

Fayetteville

Cape Fear River

WILMINGTON &

Beaufort

Cheraw

SOUTH CAROLINA

WILMINGTON & MANCHESTER RR

Columbia

NORTHEASTERN RR

Peedee River

Wilmington

FORT FISHER

ATLANTIC OCEAN

SOUTH CAROLINA RR

Augusta

Santee River

Milledgeville

Savannah River

Edisto River

CHARLESTON & SAVANNAH RR

Combahee River

Charleston

Savannah

ATLANTIC OCEAN

Scale in Miles

0   150   300

Other Publications:

THE TIME-LIFE GARDENER'S GUIDE
MYSTERIES OF THE UNKNOWN
TIME FRAME
FIX IT YOURSELF
FITNESS, HEALTH & NUTRITION
SUCCESSFUL PARENTING
HEALTHY HOME COOKING
UNDERSTANDING COMPUTERS
LIBRARY OF NATIONS
THE ENCHANTED WORLD
THE KODAK LIBRARY OF CREATIVE PHOTOGRAPHY
GREAT MEALS IN MINUTES
PLANET EARTH
COLLECTOR'S LIBRARY OF THE CIVIL WAR
THE EPIC OF FLIGHT
THE GOOD COOK
WORLD WAR II
HOME REPAIR AND IMPROVEMENT
THE OLD WEST

For information on and a full description of any of the
Time-Life Books series listed above, please call 1-800-621-
7026 or write:
Reader Information
Time-Life Customer Service
P.O. Box C-32068
Richmond, Virginia 23261-2068

This volume is one of a series that chronicles in full the
events of the American Civil War, 1861-1865.
Other books in the series include:

The Cover: Tearful veterans of the Army of Northern
Virginia furl their flag at Appomattox on April 9,
1865. "With a reluctance that was appealingly pathetic, the torn and tattered battleflags were laid upon the
ground," wrote General Joshua Chamberlain, who
accepted their surrender. "Some of the men who had
carried and followed those ragged standards through
four years of strife rushed from the ranks, bent about
their flags, and pressed them to their lips."

THE CIVIL WAR

PURSUIT TO APPOMATTOX

BY

JERRY KORN

AND THE

EDITORS OF TIME-LIFE BOOKS

The Last Battles

TIME-LIFE BOOKS, ALEXANDRIA, VIRGINIA

The Civil War
Series Director: Thomas H. Flaherty
Designer: Edward Frank
Series Administrator: Jane Edwin

Editorial Staff for *Pursuit to Appomattox*
Associate Editor: Marion F. Briggs (pictures)
Staff Writers: Janet Cave, Margery A. duMond,
John Newton, Brian C. Pohanka, Daniel Stashower,
David S. Thomson
Researchers: Harris J. Andrews, Stephanie Lewis
Assistant Designer: Lorraine D. Rivard
Copy Coordinators: Vivian Noble, Jayne E. Rohrich
Picture Coordinator: Betty H. Weatherley
Editorial Assistant: Donna Fountain
Special Contributors: Thomas A. Lewis (text),
Brian E. McGinn

Editorial Operations
Copy Chief: Diane Ullius
Editorial Operations: Caroline A. Boubin (manager)
Production: Celia Beattie
Quality Control: James J. Cox (director)
Library: Louise D. Forstall

Correspondents: Elisabeth Kraemer-Singh (Bonn);
Maria Vincenza Aloisi (Paris); Ann Natanson (Rome).
Valuable assistance was also provided by: Christina
Lieberman (New York).

The Author:
Jerry Korn won the Distinguished Flying Cross as a B-24
copilot in World War II; he then worked as a reporter for
the Associated Press before becoming an editor for *Col-
lier's* and *Life*. He served for 12 years as the managing
editor of Time-Life Books. He is also the author of *War on
the Mississippi* and *The Fight for Chattanooga* in the Time-
Life Books Civil War series.

The Consultants:
Christopher M. Calkins, Historian at the Petersburg Na-
tional Battlefield, began his career in the National Park
Service in 1971 at the Appomattox Court House National
Historic Park. He is the author of several books about the
final days of the Civil War, including *Thirty-Six Hours
before Appomattox* and *From Petersburg to Appomattox,
April 2-9, 1865*.

Colonel John R. Elting, USA (Ret.), a former Associate
Professor at West Point, is the author of *Battles for Scandi-
navia* in the Time-Life Books World War II series and of
*The Battle of Bunker's Hill, The Battles of Saratoga, Mili-
tary History and Atlas of the Napoleonic Wars, American
Army Life* and *The Superstrategists*. Co-author of *A Dic-
tionary of Soldier Talk*, he is also editor of the three vol-
umes of *Military Uniforms in America, 1755-1867*, and associate editor of *The West Point Atlas of American Wars*.

William A. Frassanito, a Civil War historian and lecturer
specializing in photograph analysis, is the author of two
award-winning studies, *Gettysburg: A Journey in Time* and
*Antietam: The Photographic Legacy of America's Bloodiest
Day*, and a companion volume, *Grant and Lee, The Virginia Campaigns*. He has also served as chief consultant to the
photographic history series *The Image of War*.

Les Jensen, Director of the Second Armored Division
Museum, Fort Hood, Texas, specializes in Civil War arti-
facts and is a conservator of historic flags. He is a contribu-
tor to *The Image of War* series, consultant for numerous
Civil War publications and museums, and a member of
the Company of Military Historians. He was formerly Curator of the U.S. Army Transportation Museum at Fort
Eustis, Virginia, and before that Curator of the Museum
of the Confederacy in Richmond, Virginia.

Michael McAfee specializes in military uniforms and has
been Curator of Uniforms and History at the West Point
Museum since 1970. A fellow of the Company of Military
Historians, he coedited with Colonel Elting *Long Endure:
The Civil War Years*, and he collaborated with Frederick
Todd on *American Military Equipage*. He is the author of
Artillery of the American Revolution, 1775-1783, and has
written numerous articles for *Military Images Magazine*.

James P. Shenton, Professor of History at Columbia University, is a specialist in 19th-century American political
and social history, with particular emphasis on the Civil
War period. He is the author of *Robert John Walker* and
Reconstruction South.

Library of Congress Cataloguing in Publication Data
Korn, Jerry.
  Pursuit to Appomattox.
  (The Civil War)
  Bibliography: p.
  Includes index.
  1. Sherman's March through the Carolinas.
2. Appomattox Campaign, 1865. 3. Virginia —
History — Civil War, 1861-1865 — Campaigns.
I. Time-Life Books.   II. Title.   III. Series.
E477.7.K67 1987   973.7'38   86-23159
ISBN 0-8094-4788-6
ISBN 0-8094-4789-4 (lib. bdg.)

CONTENTS

Poised for a Final Push

By the winter of 1865, the Army of the Potomac had recovered from its terrible sacrifices of the previous spring and summer, and the gloom that had pervaded Federal ranks after the failure to take Petersburg gave way to optimism. Although stalemated in the Petersburg-Richmond trench lines, the Federals had never relaxed their bulldog grip on Robert E. Lee's Army of Northern Virginia. As a result, Union armies elsewhere had won smashing victories: Sherman had completed his devastating march to the sea, Thomas had destroyed Hood in Tennessee and Sheridan had razed much of the Shenandoah Valley.

As the veterans of the Army of the Potomac went about camp routines, recruits poured in. "Our receipts are now considerably more than our losses," a colonel in V Corps declared. "We have not had such men enlisting since the first furor of patriotism." It was plain that an end to the war was approaching. "Everyone knew that with the advent of spring, the final struggle must occur," a cavalry captain wrote. "And few, if any, doubted what the result would be."

Troopers of the Independent Company Oneida (New York) Cavalry, the headquarters escort of the Army of the Potomac, relax outside their comfortable log huts near Petersburg in March 1865. During four years of war, the New Yorkers served all four men who, at one time or another, commanded the army: Generals George B. McClellan, Ambrose E. Burnside, Joseph Hooker — and now George G. Meade.

Artillery officers and men stand beside a bomb-proof made of sandbags and logs inside Fort Burnham, formerly Confederate Fort Harrison, southeast of Richmond. The Federals had captured the fort in September 1864 and renamed it for Brigadier General Hiram Burnham, who had been killed leading a reconnaissance just before the attack.

A horse-drawn delivery cart waits beneath a hill pocked with the tarpaulin-covered dugouts of the U.S. Colored Infantry at Dutch Gap on the James River. The crude shelters, called "gopher holes" by the men, were exposed to fire from Confederate ships and batteries.

Staff engineers gather to smoke and converse in front of one of their tents. These highly trained men were assigned to various commands within the Army of the Potomac to advise on the building of fortifications, roads and bridges.

Cavalrymen and infantry attached to the Provost Guard, the military police of the Army of the Potomac, assemble before their stockade for the morning ritual of inspection. The officer of the guard at right is examining the rifle of a soldier detailed from the 114th Pennsylvania Zouaves.

These photographs of a
V Corps captain *(left)*, an enlisted man *(above)* and three
IX Corps medical officers
(right), all posed on the same
pine bench, were taken by a
Union Army photographer at
an improvised studio near
Petersburg. The boxes
shown propped against the
bench are the photogra-
pher's printing frames, used
to duplicate maps.

Buglers and troopers of the 5th U.S. Cavalry, part of General Ulysses S. Grant's escort, stand at attention at City Point, Virginia, in March 1865. "All quiet and nothing to do but drill," one soldier wrote during the winter lull. "But business will soon be brisk enough to suit us all. This siege must end soon."

Preparing for casualties to come, stretcher-bearers of the 114th Pennsylvania Zouaves practice the loading of wounded onto an ambulance. Such drills helped to fill idle time and increased the efficiency of the reinforced Federal command.

Inside Fort Burnham, three artillerymen sit beside a 100-pounder Parrott rifle mounted on a barbette carriage, which allowed it to traverse from side to side. "I have endured this life for four years," a soldier noted in his diary in late March 1865. "Great events are to happen in a few days, and I want to be there to see the end."

A Season of Forlorn Hope

"The Union troops during the winter lay behind their works with full feeling of security, and rested and recuperated. In truth, they needed rest. The unremitting and terrific hammering of the last campaign had worn them down. They were fought out. Many gallant spirits, the soul of an army, had fallen. The loss in officers was especially heavy. The troops, jaded and depressed, obeyed orders; indeed, ever responded to the call to battle, but without confidence or vigor, as an exhausted charger moves at the prick of the spur."

MAJOR HAZARD STEVENS, VI CORPS, AT PETERSBURG

As 1864 drew to a close, a welcome report circulated among the tattered Confederates shivering in the trenches outside Petersburg and Richmond. The ladies of the Southern capital were preparing a holiday feast for their defenders. Farmers had been asked to contribute something, and the women themselves planned to carry the food up to the lines on New Year's Day.

At the very thought of this treat, said a soldier in the 18th Georgia, "our mouths watered." Food was so scarce in General Robert E. Lee's Army of Northern Virginia that Captain Watson D. Williams of the 5th Texas ruefully wrote home that he would eat his Christmas dinner from his tin cup and drink "clear cold water from a well just in the rear of the breastworks" in place of his usual eggnog. The daily ration of meat amounted to three or four ounces — scarcely more than a mouthful per man. Food boxes from home, long a supplement to the meager rations, now routinely disappeared in the collapsing Confederate transportation system.

"Starvation, literal starvation," reported Major General John B. Gordon, had so weakened his men that minor scratches often resulted in infection and even death. Enfeebled and dejected, the usually high-spirited Confederates had sunk into apathy. "I have seen stalwart men sit and brood for hours," one private said. And not only the enlisted men were going hungry. An Irish member of Parliament who visited Lee was invited to dinner. "He had two biscuits," said the visitor, "and he gave me one."

But now the Southern troops anticipated some real food. They heard that sides of beef, mutton, venison and pork had been collected and prepared under the direction of Richmond's leading caterer. Loaves of bread — a luxury — were being contributed by a local bakery. Excitement mounted.

News of the event had spread to the Federal ranks as well. Lieutenant General Ulysses S. Grant, the general in chief, had learned of the impending feast across the lines and had ordered his men to hold their fire all day. The Confederates had extended the same courtesy during a Federal celebration the previous Thanksgiving.

On the appointed day, the men in the lines awakened early. Their wait was a long one because of a shortage of transport. Noon came, and evening, and midnight; still the men waited, refusing to eat their rations.

It was past 3 a.m. on January 2 when the 18th Georgia got its share of the feast. After the food was delivered, the men stared. The labors of the Richmond women had produced, for each soldier, "one small sandwich made up of two tiny slices of bread and a thin

A trenchbound South Carolina soldier wore this woolen hood, called a balaclava, during the cold winter nights at Petersburg in 1865. The hand-knit hat was styled and named after the headgear British troops used in Russia during the Crimean War.

piece of ham." Other units received similarly scant servings. Nonetheless, murmurs of disappointment were hushed, and the Georgians ate their food thoughtfully; whatever the quantity, it was better than what they had been getting. When they were finished, a middle-aged corporal lit his pipe. "God bless our noble women," he said quietly. "It was all they could do; it was all they had."

For many of the women, in fact, it may have been more than they had for themselves. Food was as scarce in the capital as it was in the trenches. "Day by day," recalled Mrs. Sallie Putnam, "our wants and privations increased." On January 15, War Department clerk John B. Jones recorded in his diary that he had enough food — "flour, meal and beans (black)" — to sustain his family of seven for two weeks. A few days later Jones reported that he was out of wood and that he had to do his "little cooking in the parlor with the coal in the grate. This is famine!" Yet the Jones family was better off than some, who were said to be eating rats.

In the midst of this indigence, with guns rumbling continuously in the background, Richmond's citizens strove to distract themselves. With the men wearing patched, ill-fitting coats, and the women in aged or makeshift gowns, they grimly parodied their former social life. Some gave "starvation parties" — soon called, simply, "starvations" — at which the only refreshment served was James River water.

And they went to weddings. During a single week in January, Major Henry Kyd Douglas was invited to three, in Waynesboro, Staunton and Woodstock. Young Douglas was so busy he missed the wedding of the season in Richmond — that of Brigadier General John Pegram. The ceremony,

in St. Paul's Episcopal Church on January 19, was remembered — perhaps with the benefit of hindsight — for its ill omens. On the way to the church, the horses drawing the bridal carriage became unruly and the bride, a famous Baltimore beauty, tore her dress and almost lost her veil. "A superstitious murmur passed through the immense congregation," Douglas wrote later, but the celebrated couple "went on to their fate."

However bravely the socialites tried to skirt the fact, the South was in dire straits. Since 1861, the Confederacy had kept the War going by improvisation, by determination, and by the discipline, courage and élan of its fighting men. Now, after almost four years of combat, exhaustion had set in. The Confederate war effort was sagging visibly, and many people were openly defeatist.

The most obvious manifestation of the collapsing system was the swift, destructive inflation of the Confederate dollar. In 1861, one gold dollar had been equivalent to $1.03 in Confederate money; as 1865 began, a dollar in gold equaled almost $60 Confederate — and the figure was climbing rapidly. In Richmond, all prices were high and the prices of commodities in short supply were staggering. Richmonders were paying $45 Confederate for a pound of coffee, $100 for a pound of tea and $25 for a pound of butter — when those items were available at all. The price of flour was $1,250 a barrel, and rising. Inflation had struck the army, too. Tobacco, which cost from $20 to $25 a plug, had to be issued free to privates, because they were paid only $17 a month.

The sense that the Confederacy was in trouble was shared by Southerners everywhere, but the privations did not affect all regions alike. There was food in some areas, especially where there had been little fighting (and therefore no hungry armies to feed). Lieutenant John S. Wise, assigned to southwestern Virginia in the fall of 1864, said he had found it "a land of milk and honey." Dairy products were plentiful, and the butter that cost $25 a pound in Richmond was selling near the Tennessee border for eight dollars. In an obscure central Virginia village named Appomattox Court House, flour was selling for half the Richmond price.

The main problem was one of distribution. The South's railroads, few and in poor condition before 1861, had deteriorated steadily during the War. By 1865, a number of the most critical rail lines had been cut by Federal armies, and the supplies the trains had carried were denied to the immobilized Army of Northern Virginia.

The Confederate Commissary Department, notorious for its inefficiency, had been forced to import meat and other foodstuffs from abroad. The job was extremely difficult, because Federal land and naval forces had closed all but one port — Wilmington, on the Cape Fear River in North Carolina. In late 1864, the Federals had severed the Weldon Railroad, which connected Petersburg and Wilmington — thus making necessary a long trek by wagon train to get supplies around the Federal lines.

Then, on January 15, a Federal force under Brigadier General Alfred H. Terry captured Fort Fisher, at the mouth of the Cape Fear River, and closed the port of Wilmington. The Confederacy was now cut off from all sea trade with foreign countries.

The strategic situation was deteriorating hand in hand with the logistical as the winter progressed. Lee's hungry and poorly clad 65,000-man army faced Grant's 115,000 men

AMUSEMENTS.

NEW RICHMOND THEATRE,
CORNER OF SEVENTH AND BROAD STREETS.

"HAPPY NEW YEAR,"
AND
"MAY GOD BLESS US ALL!"

SATURDAY EVENING, DEC. 31, 1864,

UPON THE SAME NIGHT,
THE
ENTIRE PLAY
OF
BLACK-EYED SUSAN;
OR,
ALL IN THE DOWNS.

William..Miss Katie Estelle.
Susan...Mrs. B. Dalton.
Incidental to the piece the renowned ballad of
BLACK-EYED SUSAN,
and
A GRAND FESTIVAL DANCE
by the
ENTIRE COMPANY AND
CORPS DE BALLET.

Belinda.......................................Miss Inez Floyd.

And the operatic play of
THE DAUGHTER OF THE REGIMENT.
Josephine.................................Miss Sallie Partington.
Marchioness.....................................Mrs. O. DeBar.
See bills of the day for full cast.

This theater bill in the Richmond *Enquirer* offered New Year's Eve entertainment for residents of the beleaguered city, who were suffering from shortages of food, clothing and fuel, as well as from the impact of bad news at the front. "It is a merciful provision of Providence," a soldier on furlough observed, "which supplies diversion to mankind in the most desperate of situations."

along 37 miles of entrenchments, from White Oak Swamp (northeast of Richmond near Cold Harbor) to Hatcher's Run (southwest of Petersburg). Lieutenant General James Longstreet, still suffering from the crippling wound he had sustained in the Wilderness, held the line north of the James River with two divisions of his I Corps. South of the river II Corps, under the temporary command of General Gordon, held the center with Lieutenant General Richard H. Anderson's understrength corps. The Confederate right, stretching westward below Petersburg to where the Boydton Plank Road crossed

Hatcher's Run, was the responsibility of the ailing Lieutenant General Ambrose Powell Hill and his III Corps. Manning the Richmond forts and the lines facing Major General Edward O. C. Ord's 40,000-man Army of the James were the 5,300 men of Lieutenant General Richard Ewell's corps.

Lieutenant John Wise visited the headquarters of his father, Brigadier General Henry A. Wise, in the trenches near Hatcher's Run. The men, as he later described them, "were huddled in snow and mud, without adequate supplies of food or fuel or clothing. The struggle was no longer a test of valor in excitement: it had become one of inactive endurance." And beyond doubt, with the coming of spring, Grant would renew his slow encirclement aimed at strangling the Army of Northern Virginia.

There was yet another threat. Just before Christmas, word had come that Savannah, on the Georgia coast, had fallen to Major General William Tecumseh Sherman, after his march from Atlanta. The Carolinas, immediately to the north, were likely to be Sherman's next objective.

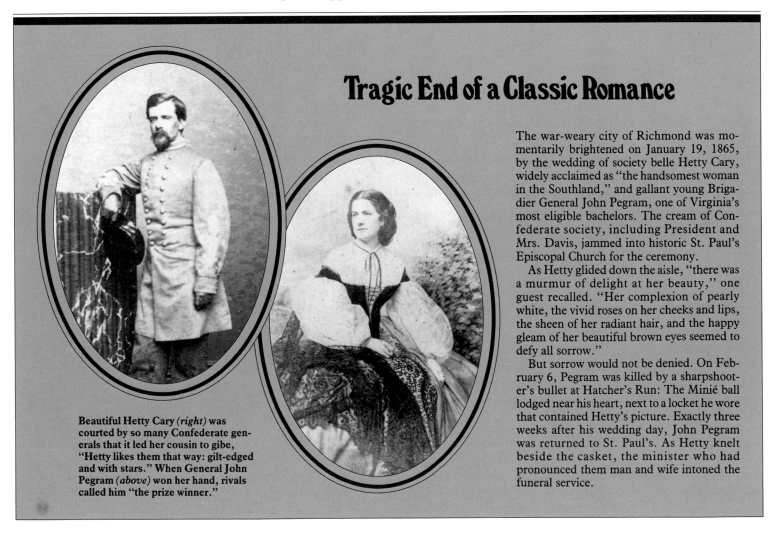

Tragic End of a Classic Romance

The war-weary city of Richmond was momentarily brightened on January 19, 1865, by the wedding of society belle Hetty Cary, widely acclaimed as "the handsomest woman in the Southland," and gallant young Brigadier General John Pegram, one of Virginia's most eligible bachelors. The cream of Confederate society, including President and Mrs. Davis, jammed into historic St. Paul's Episcopal Church for the ceremony.

As Hetty glided down the aisle, "there was a murmur of delight at her beauty," one guest recalled. "Her complexion of pearly white, the vivid roses on her cheeks and lips, the sheen of her radiant hair, and the happy gleam of her beautiful brown eyes seemed to defy all sorrow."

But sorrow would not be denied. On February 6, Pegram was killed by a sharpshooter's bullet at Hatcher's Run: The Minié ball lodged near his heart, next to a locket he wore that contained Hetty's picture. Exactly three weeks after his wedding day, John Pegram was returned to St. Paul's. As Hetty knelt beside the casket, the minister who had pronounced them man and wife intoned the funeral service.

Beautiful Hetty Cary (*right*) was courted by so many Confederate generals that it led her cousin to gibe, "Hetty likes them that way: gilt-edged and with stars." When General John Pegram (*above*) won her hand, rivals called him "the prize winner."

Of all the problems besetting the South at the beginning of 1865, perhaps the one that most worried Lee was a shortage of troops. His army was running out of soldiers, and the Confederate States had few men to replace them. The Confederate Congress started seriously to consider the extreme step of recruiting slaves as soldiers, possibly in return for their emancipation. In fact, such legislation passed in March — without the emancipation provision — and within a few days, astonished Richmonders saw black Confederates on parade in Capitol Square.

As a further measure, teenagers and men in their sixties were being enrolled in reserve units. Lieutenant Wise, assigned to such a unit, said it "presented every stage of manhood from immature boyhood to decrepit old age"; the battle line of one company, he continued, "looked as irregular as a pile of barrel-hoops." A Federal general reported taking into his lines 13-year-old deserters. But there was no real solution to the problem of troop strength. Since 1861 the Confederacy had put about 750,000 soldiers in the field; in all theaters there were now fewer than 160,000 on duty. The rest, one officer said, had been "worn out and killed out and starved out."

The worst attrition was being caused not by battle losses but by desertion, which, Lee conceded, had reached alarming proportions. Admiral Raphael Semmes, taking breakfast with Lee in late January, heard from him that 160 soldiers had deserted in a group the night before. General Grant estimated that the Southern troops were deserting at the rate of a regiment a day. And indeed, John S. Preston, Superintendant of the Conscription Bureau, reported in February that 100,000 soldiers were absent from the various Confederate armies. Many, at the urging of their loved ones, had gone home to the Carolinas to be with their families in the face of Sherman's depredations. Others simply crossed the lines and surrendered.

The Federals encouraged these desertions. With printed circulars and with word passed picket to picket, they announced repeatedly that deserters would be welcomed and that they should bring their muskets. The Federals offered eight dollars apiece for the weapons — and did such a rushing business that the Army of the Potomac had to set aside $10,000 to pay for them.

Lee did everything he could to stop the attrition. He urged President Jefferson Davis' Administration, in vain, to stop undermining discipline by pardoning deserters wholesale. "I cannot keep the army together unless examples are made of such cases," Lee wrote to the Confederate adjutant general. At the same time, Lee offered a 20-day amnesty to lure back soldiers who had abandoned the ranks. One of his corps commanders, General Longstreet, suggested offering commissions in the new black regiments to anyone who turned in deserters. Lee even tried to put an end to jokes about desertion; to suggest flight even in jest, he said in a stern order to his troops, was an offense punishable by death. The warning was read to all units for three days running.

Under the circumstances, it was not surprising that when a peace feeler arrived from the North shortly after the first of the year — even though it was proffered by a private citizen and based on a preposterous plan — the South grasped at it. The scheme had been conceived by the 74-year-old editor and politician Francis P. Blair; one of his sons

On sentry duty at sunset, a lone Federal cavalryman scans the western horizon in this painting by the soldier-artist Julian Scott. "During the last two years no branch of the Army of the Potomac contributed so much to the overthrow of Lee's army as the cavalry," conceded a Confederate officer. "But for the efficiency of this force, the War would have been indefinitely prolonged."

had served as Lincoln's first Postmaster General and another was a corps commander in Sherman's army. It was Blair's notion that the North and the South might be persuaded to stop fighting each other and instead join in attacking the French-supported government of the Emperor Maximilian in Mexico. Blair thought Jefferson Davis might serve as dictator of Mexico after the Emperor's ouster.

Although both Davis and Lincoln may have considered Blair's proposal absurd, it did offer something neither President was willing to discourage out-of-hand: an opportunity for the two sides to talk to each other on the subject of peace. Lincoln accordingly gave Blair a pass through the Federal lines (he was careful not to endorse Blair's plan — or even listen to it); and Davis gave Blair an audience in Richmond on January 12.

Blair explained his proposal and suggested

that Davis might appoint a commission to carry on further discussions. After some hesitation, Davis agreed. On January 31, the commission crossed the lines outside Petersburg, was cheered heartily by the war-weary soldiers of both sides and eventually appeared at Grant's headquarters at City Point. The commission was a distinguished group consisting of Vice President Alexander Stephens, Assistant Secretary of War John A. Campbell and Senator Robert M. T. Hunter of Virginia. The Northern Secretary of State, William H. Seward, meanwhile had been sent from Washington to talk with the three Confederates and was awaiting them at Fort Monroe in Hampton Roads.

There was a problem, however, in getting the discussions under way. The Confederate commissioners had instructions from Davis not to meet with anyone unless it was ex-

The Most Comfortable Camp in the Army

While the Federal infantry outside Petersburg endured the elements in crude, makeshift shelters, the engineers behind the lines lived in comparative luxury. Especially comfortable were the 50th New York Volunteer Engineers, whose winter quarters at Poplar Grove were the envy of the Army of the Potomac. "In erecting them," an admiring infantryman wrote, "they gave their mechanical skill full play."

The New Yorkers began by clearing a substantial area of pine and white oak trees in order to form a parade ground. Then they used the downed timber to construct a small village of neat, Gothic-style cottages. Regimental artisans gave the camp a decidedly homey appearance with some extra touches, such as shingle roofs, ornamental fences and corduroyed sidewalks.

The engineers' masterwork was a handsome rustic church (*opposite*) built of pine logs squared on three sides with the bark left on the outer side. Its towering steeple was fashioned from saplings about one and a half inches in diameter. Inside, the church boasted a dais that — on evenings other than the Sabbath — was used as a stage for amateur theatricals. The performances attracted enthusiastic audiences from rival commands for miles around.

The 50th New York's headquarters borders a spotless parade ground. "We have a beautiful camp," an engineer wrote. "Nothing compares with it."

Officers of the 50th New York Volunteer Engineers assemble in front of the church they erected near the site of the old Poplar Grove Meeting House, southeast of Petersburg. On the façades of the church and the storage building *(above)* is a small turreted castle, the symbol of the Engineering Corps. This device, in the form of a brass insignia *(inset)*, was worn by the men on their forage caps.

When the engineers finally broke camp in April 1865, they left behind a wooden tablet presenting their church to the meetinghouse trustees.

pressly understood that they represented an independent nation. Lincoln, on the other hand, had made it clear that no such understanding was acceptable. He had, after all, taken the country to war four years earlier on the principle that the Union was indissoluble; from the Northern point of view there was no Confederate nation, merely a section of the Union that was in rebellion. The three commissioners struggled to find some compromise wording acceptable to both Presidents, but nothing sufficed: Every proposal was rejected by the Administration in Washington, where the negotiations were being overseen by the dour Secretary of War, Edwin M. Stanton. It seemed that the Confederates would have to return to Richmond.

When the three Southerners had appeared on his doorstep, Grant had given them comfortable accommodations and the run of City Point; several relaxed and friendly conversations had taken place. Grant thought the Southerners sincere, and when it appeared that their undertaking was about to founder, he decided to lend a hand. Keeping in mind that he was a military officer dabbling in political affairs, Grant sent a careful message to Stanton expressing regret that President Lincoln could not meet in person with the Confederate trio. The message was intended, of course, for the President, and Lincoln responded at once: If Grant wanted him, he would come. "Say to the gentlemen," he wired, "I will meet them personally at Fortress Monroe as soon as I can get there."

And so it happened that on February 3, the Union President and the Secretary of State met the Confederate commissioners in the saloon of the steamer *River Queen* in Hampton Roads and talked peace. The meeting lasted four hours and accomplished

A *carte de visite* featuring President Lincoln and his top commanders was circulated in the North, as a mocking response to Confederate peace feelers, in early 1865. Scenting victory, the Unionists maintained that arms alone would settle the conflict.

nothing. Lincoln made clear that restoration of the Union was one prerequisite to peace and acceptance of the abolition of slavery another. He informed the Confederates that the United States Congress had just passed the 13th Amendment to the Constitution, which put an end to slavery, and that the amendment had already been submitted to the Northern states for ratification.

The rigidity of Lincoln's insistence that there was no Confederate nation took the Southerners aback. Incredulous, Senator Hunter tried to get a fix on the Northern leader's position. "Mr. President," he said, "if we understand you correctly, you think we of the Confederacy have committed treason; that we are traitors to your government; that we have forfeited our rights, and are proper subjects for the hangman. Is that not about what your words imply?"

There was a long, thoughtful pause. "Yes," said Lincoln at last. "You have stated the proposition better than I did. That is about the size of it."

Yet the meeting was cordial, and after the Southerners left, Seward sent a rowboat after them; the black man at the oars carried a bottle of champagne as a farewell gift to the commissioners. In the stern of the *River Queen* stood Seward with a speaking trumpet. "Keep the champagne," he shouted across the water, "but return the Negro!"

Jefferson Davis reacted defiantly to the news of the rebuff. He referred scornfully to "His Majesty Abraham the First" and predicted that the Union would soon be forced to "petition us for peace, on our terms." It was sheer bravado from a man who appeared to be losing his grip on the War, on his presidency — and perhaps on reality.

The Confederate Congress had progressed from discontent to anger to open rebellion over Davis' brand of leadership. Davis' conduct of the War and his contentious relationship with some of his generals were bitterly assailed; his autocratic manner further angered many of his supporters and opponents alike. Many Congressmen despised his chief military adviser, Braxton Bragg, who was perhaps the most disliked general in the Confederacy. Only Lee and his army seemed exempt from the President's meddling.

On February 6, the day Davis announced the failure of the peace initiative, he made official two major changes that were intended to bolster his increasingly shaky tenure in office and to revitalize the Confederate war effort. With as much good grace as he could muster, considering that the Congress had forced him to do it, Davis issued an order making Lee general in chief of the Confederate armed forces. The unstated corollary to this belated appointment was that Davis' personal military staff would be disbanded.

On the same day, in response to a demand from Virginia's influential congressional delegation, a new Secretary of War took office to replace the exhausted and embittered James Seddon. Davis brought in Major General John C. Breckinridge, a former Vice President of the United States and an experienced commander whose career had suffered after he got on the wrong side of Braxton Bragg during the Tennessee Campaign. Breckinridge took firm control of the War Department, effecting immediate improvement in its organization and, more important, in the movement of food and supplies to the Army of Northern Virginia.

Congressional pressure also brought reform to the Commissary Department. The unpopular Commissary General Lucius Northrop was eased out and, with Senate approval, replaced by Brigadier General Isaac M. St. John, who found his new department in chaos. The plight of a Confederate quartermaster in Alabama was typical: "We suffer a total want of funds. Owing to this, all the branches of the service are at a standstill, transportation is embarrassed, supplies slowly and with difficulty obtained, and impressments also totally impossible." Even the arrival at Wilmington in December of 950,000 rations of meat from Nassau had helped only a little; the narrow-gauge Weldon Railroad from Wilmington, its rolling stock depleted, could move only part of the food. But in January, when Lee issued a per-

IMPETUOUS CHARGE OF THE FIRST COLORED REBEL REGIMENT.
[By our Prophetic Artist.]

sonal appeal to the people of Virginia, enough food was donated to feed his hungry army for a few more days.

St. John quickly instituted reforms in the distribution of supplies to men in the field, and his efforts — combined with the static position of the Army of Northern Virginia — began to improve the soldiers' lot. The coming of spring would bring the issue of new uniforms to many of the threadbare troops. St. John also managed to assemble a reserve of 3 million rations of bread and 2.5 million rations of meat.

Lee used his new authority as general in chief to put General Joseph E. Johnston, another casualty of Davis' venomous dislike, back in command of the forces facing Sherman, who by that time was in Columbia, South Carolina, and edging northward. All of the new reforms were changes for the better, yet there was a pervasive sense that they had come too late.

One other attempt to end the War by negotiation occurred on February 21. Generals Longstreet and Ord met between the lines under a flag of truce to discuss the fraterniza-tion between pickets, a problem for both armies. The talk turned to the need for peace. Ord proposed that perhaps the generals could end the fighting by a straightforward military convention, leaving it to the statesmen to clean up the details. Again the Confederacy grasped at the straw. Lee, with Davis' approval, wrote to Grant suggesting that they meet to discuss peace arrangements. Grant immediately forwarded the communication to Washington. The reply, signed by Stanton but written by Lincoln, was unequivocal. Grant was not to meet with Lee unless it was to discuss Lee's capitulation: "You are not to decide, discuss, or confer upon any political question. Such questions the President holds in his own hands, and will submit them to no military conferences or conventions. Meantime you are to press to the utmost your military advantages."

That reply ended the peace moves. It was now clear to both sides that the War would have to be fought to a military conclusion.

The fighting had, in fact, been going on during the peace talks. The winter had been unusually harsh — rain and mud alternating

TO THE CITIZENS OF
LYNCHBURG AND CAMPBELL CO.

LYNCHBURG, February 28th, 1865.

The undersigned, by authority of the Commissary General, solicits IMMEDIATE supplies for the army, of BACON, PORK, BEEF, FLOUR, WHEAT, CORN, CORN MEAL, BEANS, PEAS and DRIED FRUIT—either as donations, loans or sales. The department gives assurance that loans will be returned in kind as soon as practicable, and all purchases will be paid for in Government Certificates which, by a recent and special act of Congress, are redeemable in taxes.

The undersigned have full authority to fix the prices of all articles delivered in their district, which will be determined in reference to the fair market and not schedule rates. They are prepared to make contracts for future as well as present deliveries.

OUR ARMY IS IN WANT—Nothing further need be said to a Virginian.

JOHN ROBIN McDANIEL,
BOLING CLARK,
RICHARD MORGAN.

This broadside, part of a campaign begun by the new Confederate Commissary chief, General Isaac St. John, to feed Lee's army, brought immediate results. Officials reported that depots were "rapidly filling up with flour, meal, corn and bacon."

with snow and ice — yet Grant dared not wait until spring to get his men on the move. His objective was not merely to take Petersburg and Richmond, but to destroy the Army of Northern Virginia. "I was afraid, every morning," he later admitted, "that I would awake from my sleep to hear that Lee had gone, and that nothing was left but a picket line." If Lee could escape into the western mountains, the War might go on for months.

One way to fix Lee in position was to keep him occupied; Grant therefore scheduled an offensive operation to begin on February 5. The move was also meant to continue the slow encirclement of Lee's army, which had been Grant's strategy for nine months, and of restricting even more the flow of supplies to the besieged Confederates.

By the end of 1864, the Federals had extended their entrenchments to just beyond the Boydton Plank Road, about eight miles west of the Weldon Railroad and 10 miles southwest of Petersburg. The Confederates, desperate to shield the Southside Railroad — their one remaining link to the West and South — had thrown up an additional seven

miles of fortifications on a line that bent southwestward to Hatcher's Run, then to the northwest, parallel to the stream and across the Boydton Plank Road.

Grant believed that the Boydton road was being used heavily by enemy wagon trains carrying supplies north from the interrupted Weldon Railroad. He sent Colonel J. Irvin Gregg's cavalry division southwest to Dinwiddie Court House — on the plank road six miles southwest of the Confederate line — to intercept and destroy as much of the traffic as he could. Following Grant's directive, Major General George G. Meade, commanding the Army of the Potomac, ordered Major General Gouverneur K. Warren to place his V Corps a few miles east of Dinwiddie to support Gregg. And to prevent the Confederates from cutting off Gregg and V Corps, two divisions of Major General Andrew A. Humphreys' II Corps moved beyond the entrenched Federal left and threatened the Confederate line in the vicinity of Hatcher's Run. The Federals used the Vaughan road, a thoroughfare that ran west from the Weldon Railroad to Dinwiddie Court House.

Meade had no plans to involve his infantry, but Lee did not know that. When he learned of the Federal movements, Lee feared for the safety of the Southside Railroad, which ran from Petersburg west to Lynchburg and connected with the Richmond & Danville to North Carolina. Lee had good reason to worry: A full-scale assault over the same ground in October had been stopped only after savage fighting.

On February 5, in icy weather, the Federal infantry divisions reached their new positions and Gregg's men galloped onto the Boydton Plank Road. They found it virtually deserted. Grant had been misled by faulty

Three regiments of V Corps infantry, including the 4th Delaware, whose tattered colors and their guard are shown at right, open fire on the Confederate works *(below)* near Dabney's Saw Mill, on February 5, 1865. The Federals soon forded the creek and drove off the Confederates.

Brevet Brigadier General J. Irvin Gregg, in temporary command of the 2nd Cavalry Division, was wounded while charging Confederate infantry at Gravelly Run on February 6. "The enemy," he noted, "was too strongly posted to be dislodged by cavalry."

intelligence, and Gregg captured only a few wagons and a handful of prisoners.

Private James L. Bowen of the 37th Massachusetts Infantry recalled that his regiment marched and countermarched for hours on the narrow, frozen roads. Then the word came to dig in, and the men of the 37th set to work constructing rifle pits. It was, said Bowen, a task, "which they had acquired the faculty for doing with great rapidity. Large trees were cut down, the trunks trimmed and rolled into place, while other squads in the detail very quickly threw against them an embankment of earth suffi-

cient to resist even cannonshot. Then a 'head-log' was put in position and the work was complete." All along the Federal line, thousands of men were doing the same.

Lee in the meantime had reinforced A. P. Hill's corps on the right with two divisions from John Gordon's corps, which was next in line. In midafternoon, divisions commanded by Major General Henry Heth and Brigadier General Clement A. Evans moved south toward Hatcher's Run, with instructions to engage the nearest Federals.

For some time, the men of Brigadier General Thomas A. Smyth's II Corps division

watched the Confederates forming in front of them as they hastened to complete their barricades. At 3:45 p.m. Confederate artillery broke the stillness of the frigid woods, and as the shells crashed into the Federal works, the battle lines of Heth and Evans advanced. Evans drove straight ahead; Heth moved toward open ground to the right of the Federal line, hoping to flank Smyth and draw him out of his entrenchments. But the Confederates found their way blocked by a Federal brigade commanded by Colonel Robert D. McAllister, and after a sharp exchange, both Heth and Evans fell back to their own line.

Impressed by the enemy's strength, the Federals concentrated along Hatcher's Run, and Meade ordered in substantial reinforcements: Brigadier General Frank Wheaton's division from VI Corps and Brigadier General John F. Hartranft's division from IX Corps. The two armies watched each other uneasily until the next afternoon. Then General Warren upped the ante, sending the divisions of Major Generals Samuel Crawford and Romeyn B. Ayres to probe northwest along Hatcher's Run. Crawford led, with the stream to his right and Gregg's cavalry screening his left. The Federals advanced into terrain ominously similar to the Wilderness battlefield of the previous spring. The ground was a series of ridges with marshes in the low spots and thick stands of pines alternating with brush-choked hardwood scrub. It would be a hellish place to fight.

The Federals had not gone far before Gregg's cavalry was attacked near Gravelly Run by a brigade from General Pegram's division. Two of Pegram's other brigades advanced from the northwest and struck Crawford southeast of Dabney's Mill, a steam-powered lumber operation. The Federals

stood fast and sent Pegram's men reeling back. Ayres's division came up to help Crawford, but Lee was funneling in reinforcements faster than Warren could. Lee ordered in a division commanded by Brigadier General Joseph Finegan to support Pegram, and Evans' arrival swelled the Confederate force at Dabney's Mill to three divisions.

The Federals facing them were suffering from extremes of inexperience and fatigue. Some regiments of draftees and bounty men stumbled into combat for the first time at Dabney's Mill, while others were too fought out to function effectively. Many of Crawford's units were gravely short of ammunition and none had been brought up. When the men of Colonel Henry A. Morrow's brigade faltered, Morrow placed himself at the front of the line, shouting for the soldiers to take heart and advance. Captain James Coey of the 147th New York rode up to join Morrow, seizing his regiment's colors as he came. With a cheer the Federals went forward again, only to encounter a water-filled ditch that was too wide to cross. Morrow's ranks thinned rapidly as his men exhausted their

Brothers William and Bennett Spach, privates in the 1st Battalion, North Carolina Sharpshooters, were both taken prisoner near Dabney's Saw Mill. William, however, was incorrectly reported by the commander of his battalion as having "deserted to the Army of the Potomac."

cartridge boxes and ran to the rear.

In desperation Morrow led his men back to the edge of a grove, where he ordered them to entrench and face the enemy with bayonets and shovels. But the pressure was too great. Coey fell, shot in the face; he regained consciousness and, despite his wound, tried vainly to rally his men. Morrow was also injured in the retreat.

The rout was especially embarrassing to a veteran of the 20th Maine, a proud old regiment in V Corps. He wrote later of "how we got frightened and 'skedaddled' back through the woods like a flock of frightened sheep." A disgusted Federal officer reported that the men ran "more than a mile," although they were not even being chased.

The Confederates too showed their vulnerability when Brigadier General Charles Griffin's V Corps divisions counterattacked their onrushing line. "The enemy broke at the first volley," noted Colonel Horatio Sickel, commanding Griffin's first brigade, "and left the field in great disorder."

During this charge, the final encounter of the day, the Confederates suffered a poi-gnant loss. Major Henry Kyd Douglas described the moment: "General Pegram was shot through the body near the heart. I jumped from my horse and caught him as he fell and with assistance took him from his horse. He died in my arms, almost as soon as he touched the ground."

That evening, Colonel William H. Stewart of the 61st Virginia recalled, "The men hastily threw up scant breastworks, and as night was fast approaching made brush shelters to protect themselves as much as possible from the rain, snow and sleet; but no fires could be allowed in such close proximity to the enemy. During the evening the cooks brought to the men in the line of battle a small pone of bread each, the first morsel since early morning." The woods, wrote Stewart, were covered "with long icicles hanging from the tree limbs, which bent under the burden like weeping willows, and the cold north wind was chilling and terrible to withstand."

The confusing and inconclusive engagement had cost the Confederates a thousand casualties and the Federals twice that many; it had accomplished little beyond keeping Lee occupied. In the days after the battle, the Federals extended their entrenchments more than three miles, to the Vaughan road crossing of Hatcher's Run. The extensions had little effect on the Confederates, who were already so stretched out, Gordon noted, that in his part of the line the men were standing 15 feet apart. If Lee had needed troops from his extreme left to support those on the far right, 37 miles away, it would have taken a two-day march to get them there.

There was some question, also, about whether many of the Confederates were capable of a two-day march. The shortage of food had grown worse. On February 8, Lee

Brigadier General Charles Griffin, a career soldier who commanded V Corps's 1st Division, is flanked by his staff outside a wall tent displaying the division's flag. "General Griffin was always cool, quiet and precise," one officer recalled. "He always knew exactly where every one of his brigades, or even regiments, was."

Brigadier General G. Moxley Sorrel was shot in the lung while leading his Georgians at Hatcher's Run. "I was down this time for good," he recalled, "the breath gushing through the orifices instead of its natural channel." Sorrel survived, but fought no more.

Swarming through the woods, the Federal V Corps's 3rd Division drives the enemy from behind a rail fence on February 7. The Confederates retreated to their original line near Dabney's Saw Mill, ending the battle.

sent a bitter message to Breckinridge, the newly appointed Confederate Secretary of War. For 72 hours, he said — including "the most inclement day of the winter" — his forces had been in the lines either fighting or preparing to fight. "Some of the men have been without meat for three days," Lee reported, "and all are suffering from reduced rations and scant clothing, exposed to battle, cold, hail and sleet." Unless something could be done quickly to rectify this situation, Lee warned, "you must not be surprised if calamity befalls us."

The Federals were at that moment preparing to inflict just such a calamity, as Lee was well aware: His scouts were reporting preparations for a major enemy offensive. It seemed unlikely that the haggard, outnumbered Confederates could halt a determined Union drive; if they could not, the end might be at hand. "If Grant once breaks through our lines," observed a Confederate general, "we might as well go back to Father Abraham and say, 'Father, we have sinned.' "

The only place Lee could look for help was to South Carolina, where Johnston's army was stationed; and as it was, Johnston did not have enough men to stop Sherman. Lee's inclination was to evacuate the trap at Petersburg — a plan put forth by Longstreet late in February — and march rapidly to join Johnston. But the Confederate government would never willingly allow him to abandon Richmond. Instead, Lee resolved to do what he had done in many similar crises during three hard years: Attack. He would find a vital spot in the Federal line, concentrate all the forces he could there, punch through and clear out at least a portion of the Federal entrenchments. With a shorter line to defend, he could detach a force to go to Johnston's aid, beat Sherman, then return with Johnston to Richmond and deal with Grant.

Lee — ever the realist, the canny assessor of his opponent's resources and abilities — was suffering from an uncharacteristic spell of wishful thinking. The assumption that his starving men and emaciated horses could cover the distances and fight the battles required by his plan was dubious enough. But the idea that Grant, with his overwhelming numbers and well-known determination, would shorten his lines in response to a Confederate thrust was pure daydream.

Nevertheless, at the beginning of March, Lee called in Gordon — at 32, the youngest of his corps commanders — and asked him to find a likely place to batter through the enemy defenses. The Confederates must fight,

Gordon reported Lee as saying, because to stand still was death.

It was three weeks before Gordon came back with a detailed proposal. Near the center of the Federal line — east of Petersburg and almost a mile south of the Appomattox River — was a strong point named Fort Stedman. It was located at a place where the opposing entrenchments lay only 150 yards apart and the pickets were close enough, said Henry Kyd Douglas, "that a boy with a strong arm could have thrown a stone from the works of one into the works of the other." Fort Stedman was, in fact, so near to the Confederate positions that it was difficult to keep in repair because of sniper fire. Still, it was a formidable position, bristling with cannon, strongly manned and fronted by breast-high fraises — angled rows of sharpened logs set in the ground about six inches apart and reinforced with telegraph wire.

Gordon, pressed by his commanding general and increasingly aware of the Confederacy's bleak prospects, proposed to strike Fort Stedman with one of the most complicated assaults of the War. Before a predawn jump-off, Gordon's men would carefully clear the chevaux-de-frise from in front of their lines, trying not to alert the nearby Federal pickets. Confederate pickets, meanwhile, would stalk their enemy counterparts, getting as close as possible so that they could overwhelm the Federals quickly. The attack would be led by 50 men with axes, who would chop through fraises and abatis protecting the fort. After the axmen would come three detachments of 100 men, each detachment with a special assignment.

During his extensive observation of the Federal lines, Gordon had determined that behind Stedman were three redoubts, which commanded the fort; they had to be taken quickly or the attempt at breaking through would fail. Since Gordon believed the redoubts could not be assailed from the front, he planned to send his three detachments, each led by a guide familiar with the terrain, through the Federal lines. Pretending to be Federal soldiers fleeing the attack, they would then converge on the redoubts from behind. While they were thus engaged, the main attack force, in three columns, would take Fort Stedman and the trenches to the left and right of it. Once these strong points were neutralized, Confederate cavalry could slash through toward the Federal rear.

Gordon convinced not only himself but also General Lee that this elaborate scheme could work. "The tremendous possibility," Gordon wrote later, "was the disintegration of the whole left wing of the Federal army, or at least the dealing of such a staggering blow upon it as would disable it temporarily, enabling us to withdraw from Petersburg in safety and join Johnston in North Carolina."

There seemed to be all kinds of possibilities to the war-drugged Confederates. Some thought the infantry might drive through to Grant's military railroad, about a mile east of Stedman, and cut off supplies to the Federal left. Officers even speculated that the cavalry might ride to City Point, eight miles away, and capture Grant himself.

The attack was set for 4 a.m. on March 25. Lee augmented Gordon's corps until the youthful general was commanding four and a half divisions — almost half of the Confederate forces in front of Petersburg. And Lee promised to supply even more men, if he could move them in time from distant parts of the line. This would be a maximum effort; if it worked, the Confederates told them-

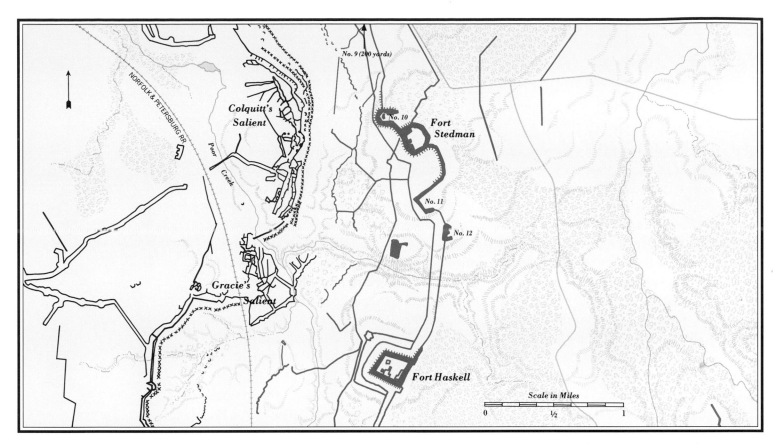

The nearness of Federal Fort Stedman to the Confederate lines at Colquitt's Salient convinced General Gordon that this was the ideal site for his attempt to break through the Union siege lines at Petersburg. Striking before dawn on March 29, Gordon's men captured the fort and the adjoining batteries: Nos. 10, 11 and 12. Nonetheless, a spirited Federal defense halted the attackers in the trenches to the north of Fort Stedman and at Fort Haskell, to the south, turning the assault into a costly Confederate defeat.

selves, it might turn the entire War around.

In its first moments, the assault succeeded beyond Gordon's expectations. Brigadier General Gaston Lewis' North Carolina brigade had detailed its own axmen, led by Lieutenant W. W. Flemming of the 57th North Carolina, to head the brigade's assault party. The 57th's colonel, Hamilton C. Jones, recorded, "Away in the East there was a band of white light in the sky which marked the approach of day. Suddenly there rang out in the stillness the sharp crack of a pistol. Instantly the enemy's pickets fired and there was a muffled sound of feet where Lieutenant Flemming's party was. Then came the rush and the rapid sound of axes and the crash of falling timber and the wild cheer from the axemen. The two regiments were at their heels and followed rapidly."

"We promptly crossed over our own works," recalled another North Carolinian, Private William M. Day of the 49th Regiment, "and whirling the *cheveaux-de-frise* around where it had not been removed, went across the field at quick step, stumbling over

and into the rifle pits that came in the way. Although under no direct fire, numbers of our men were killed. A minnie ball struck me on the ankle with a force that would have broken it, had it not been for my thick shoe." Despite the pain, Private Day kept going and, he wrote, "was soon in my place in the line again driving at the Yankee stockades, which had not been cut away in our immediate front. We had considerable difficulty in getting over, the points of the stockades striking us about the breasts. The men pulled and snatched at the sharp rails trying to break them. When they could not break them, they helped each other over. Being young and active I did not need any help, and catching the point of the rails, and giving a spring, landed on my side on top of the stockade, tearing a great hole in my blanket. I was on my feet in an instant, and all together with a rush we entered the Yankee breastworks."

The Federal pickets had received little warning, and most were taken by surprise. They had become so accustomed to seeing large groups of deserters moving through the lines, muskets in hand, that they assumed the attackers were simply coming in to give up and sell their weapons.

The pickets had time to fire one volley and the trench guards little more than that before they were overwhelmed. A Confederate grabbed Private Edward Carney, a picket of the 29th Massachusetts, by the neck and ordered him to surrender. "I don't see it!" shouted Carney, who pulled away from his would-be captor. Although a second Confederate struck Carney repeatedly in the back with his musket butt, the determined Federal rushed away into the darkness.

The main Confederate attack, in three columns, punched through the Federal line just north of Fort Stedman, between Batteries Nos. 9 and 10. While the left column moved north toward Battery 9, the other two assaulted Battery 10 and Stedman itself.

The Confederates were moving so quietly and quickly that minutes after they had seized Battery 10, a confused Federal soldier standing guard nearby was still reporting "No attack." When some Federal troops opened fire, their officers stopped them, believing they were firing into their own pickets. Colonel Napoleon B. McLaughlen, the Union commander responsible for the Fort Stedman line, rushed into the fort on hearing the firing. "I crossed the parapet," recalled McLaughlen, "and meeting some men coming over the curtains, whom in the darkness I supposed to be a part of the picket, I established them inside the work, giving directions with regard to position and firing, all of which were instantly obeyed." Moments later, it dawned on McLaughlen that the men were Confederates. They realized he was a Federal — and took him prisoner.

Battery 10 opened in the rear onto ground that was as high as Fort Stedman's parapet, giving the Confederates yet another advantage. But the fort's garrison — a portion of the 14th New York Heavy Artillery under Captain George M. Randall — had time to brace for the attack, and the New Yorkers poured a galling fire into the Confederates moving against them from Battery 10. The attackers were driven back but soon came on again from the front, flank and rear. In desperation Randall commanded his men to use bayonets and clubbed rifles as the Confederates poured over the works. "It was rough-and-tumble fighting," Major William H. Hodgkins of Massachusetts wrote later; the men were frequently "locked together like serpents," and grappling "as if they had drunk two quarts of brandy."

The defenders of Fort Stedman were overpowered, and many were captured; despite the darkness and the confusion, the remaining men refused to panic. Most fell back to the east and continued firing into the rear of the fort; others moved south along the trenches past Batteries Nos. 11 and 12 to Fort Haskell, about 600 yards away. Randall had dispatched runners to warn the flanking regiments, and the 29th and 57th Massachusetts were beginning to fall in. Meanwhile, a select team of Confederate artillerists under Lieutenant Colonel Robert M. Stribling took over the guns in Stedman and Battery 10, opening a ferocious enfilading fire on entrenchments to the north and south.

The attacking Confederates, the bulk of whom were Brigadier General Matthew W. Ransom's North Carolinians, moved north and caught the 57th Massachusetts still trying to call in its pickets. Struck in the flank and rear, many of the Massachusetts men

Three hundred infantrymen, a select force from Major General John B. Gordon's corps, pour through openings cut by axmen in the barriers shielding Fort Stedman. "Although it required but a few minutes to reach the Union works," Gordon wrote, "those minutes were to me like hours of suspense and breathless anxiety."

Captains R. D. Funkhauser (*top left*) and Joseph M. Anderson (*bottom left*) of the 49th Virginia were among the officers of Gordon's corps who spearheaded the attack on Fort Stedman. Anderson suffered a mortal wound from a Federal sentry's bullet early in the fighting. Funkhauser reached the earthworks, only to be pinned down by fire from nearby batteries. When the Federals reclaimed the fort, he was taken prisoner, along with nearly 2,000 other Confederates.

were captured, but others fought from their traverses and communication trenches. The Federals managed to form a battle line, perpendicular to their works and anchored on Battery 9. There they made a stand.

The Confederates assailing the battery were forced to take shelter 500 yards from their objective. Now they found themselves in the same situation Federal troops had faced at the Crater the previous summer. The Federal entrenchments were a maze of main-line earthworks, connecting trenches, traverses and dugouts. It was nearly impossible for the attackers to determine their position or to maintain formation.

It was the Federal left that Gordon particularly wanted to clear, and with the coming of daylight, the full fury of his onslaught was directed at Fort Haskell. The right column had already begun pressing cautiously toward Haskell from Fort Stedman, and in the early-morning gloom, the full mass of Confederates from Evans' division moved down the trenches, seizing Batteries 11 and 12 and pushing back the 29th Massachu-

setts. The 29th's color sergeant, Conrad Homan, was surrounded, but he escaped with his colors in the confusion. In Fort Haskell, Captain Christian Woerner saw an oncoming body of men, but as it was still too dark to see who they were, Woerner withheld his fire. When the men were 100 yards away, he recognized them as the enemy and ordered three of his four Napoleons to open fire. Murderous canister charges ripped into the Confederates and the assault was halted. The surviving attackers went to ground among the Federal bombproofs and winter huts.

The guns of the Confederate main line joined the captured Federal pieces in bombarding Fort Haskell; Federal field batteries and the artillerists operating the huge siege guns in the rear opened a massive counterfire. The air was so full of shells, noted Lieutenant Julius G. Tuerk of the 3rd New Jersey Artillery, that the missiles resembled "a flock of blackbirds with blazing tails beating about in a gale." Many of Fort Haskell's defenders were hit, and the Union flag was shot away. When the flag disappeared, Federal

The 3rd Division of IX Corps, made up of Pennsylvania regiments and led by Brigadier General John F. Hartranft *(inset)*, launches the charge that retook Fort Stedman on March 25. The Confederates, recalled Hartranft, "were forced back into the works in such masses that the victors were scarcely able to deploy among the crowds of their prisoners."

gunners assumed that the fort had fallen and opened fire on it. Urgently, an officer called for volunteers to hold the flag aloft. Eight men responded. Four were quickly shot down, but the survivors managed to signal the cannoneers, who ceased firing.

"We thought we had won a great victory," said Captain R. D. Funkhauser of the 49th Virginia, which had been one of Pegram's regiments, "but after daylight the enemy's guns from Fort Haskell and the commanding hills made our captured fort untenable, and we became badly demoralized so that it was with the greatest difficulty that the generals got the men in line to charge the second line of works." Funkhauser tried to get his men to attack toward Fort Haskell. "In my first attempt to lead, having to jump a ditch, only three men followed me. I was knocked down by the concussion of a shell and that brave trio started to carry me back, supposing my wound to be mortal as I was gasping

for breath; but when another shell burst nearby, they let me fall, which caused my breath to come back." Funkhauser followed his companions to safety in a bombproof.

General Gordon, who had reached Fort Stedman close behind his men, sent a message to Lee saying that all was going well. Though Gordon was unaware of it, however, his attack was in trouble. The Confederate cavalry had never advanced; the way was not open. The three 100-man detachments had quickly pressed toward the rear, but they had never found the three redoubts. The men had become separated from their guides and were wandering about in confusion. Many of the famished Southerners in and around Fort Stedman found it impossible to resist the Federal rations they saw lying about; instead of fighting, they paused to fill their stomachs.

Slowly the massive Federal army facing Petersburg was coming to life. The responsi-

bility for defending the first seven miles of Federal trenches south of the Appomattox River belonged to Major General John G. Parke's IX Corps. Parke had been startled that morning not only by the attack, but by the discovery that, while General Meade was temporarily away at City Point, he was the acting commander of the Army of the Potomac. Yet Parke reacted decisively. He had two divisions already on the line: Brigadier General Orlando B. Willcox was defending the line at Fort Stedman and Brigadier General Robert Potter was holding the trenches to the south. Porter immediately called on General Hartranft's reserve division to move toward the breach and also directed Colonel John C. Tidball's reserve artillery to take position on a ridge east of Fort Stedman.

As Hartranft's men moved forward, they encountered and drove back the three special Confederate detachments, who were still milling around in the maze behind the Federal trenches. Tidball's artillery went into battery and opened fire on the stalled Confederate main force, which was now confined to Fort Stedman and a few hundred yards of adjoining trench. More Federal reinforcements were on the way, from V and II Corps. General Gordon recalled that to his dismay the surrounding hills "were soon black with troops." By 8 a.m., four hectic hours after the attack had begun, the Confederate situation seemed hopeless, and Lee sent orders for withdrawal. At the same time, the entire Federal cordon that had been thrown around the attackers began to advance.

Gordon faced a new problem. The ground between the Confederate and Federal lines was under such blistering fire that it would be as perilous for the Confederates in the fort to return to their own lines as to stay where they were. Most did go back, risking the fire. But hundreds of others simply surrendered, disregarding the orders—and even the threats—of their officers.

A Michigan captain, glancing toward the recaptured underground headquarters of the 57th Massachusetts, saw an enemy soldier peeking out. When he went over to take the man prisoner, he found 35 Confederates in the bombproof. He took them all.

The Confederate losses in the attack on Fort Stedman had been heavy: 1,600 men killed or wounded and, remarkably, about 1,900 taken prisoner. The Federals lost only 1,000 troops, half of them prisoners. The Union forces had handled Lee's last, best effort to break their hold on Petersburg with ease. A single corps had contained and then repelled the attack. Grant, who was planning a major offensive of his own a few days later, did not bother to alter his plans. The only change in Federal activities was that a divisional review scheduled for that morning was put off until the afternoon.

A Confederate prisoner was amazed to see the review under way as he was led off. By chance, Abraham Lincoln was there, and the prisoner marveled that the President and Grant "rode by us seemingly not the least concerned and as if nothing had happened." Before this colossal self-assurance, the Confederate said, all the Southerners present understood their situation, "and with one accord agreed that our cause was lost."

Once the review was over, Lincoln himself saw a bit of the day's fighting. The President, accompanied by Mrs. Lincoln, had arrived on March 2 in response to an invitation from Grant. "I would like very much to see you," Grant had wired, "and I think the rest

Sergeant Francis M. McMillen (*left*), color-bearer of the 110th Ohio, was shot in the chest when his division attacked entrenched Confederate pickets opposite Fort Fisher, six miles southwest of Fort Stedman, during the fighting on March 25. McMillen's life was saved by a diary (*below*) in his breast pocket. An enemy Minié ball passed through the diary and turned downward, denting his pocket watch; the twisted piece of lead then hit the corner of his belt buckle, where it finally came to rest. Years later, McMillen recorded the miraculous event in his damaged diary, on the page allocated for March 25, 1865.

would do you good." Neither of them, of course, had expected the visit to be highlighted by a Confederate offensive.

Lincoln first learned of the Confederate attack from his 21-year-old son Robert, recently appointed a captain on Grant's staff. The young man had visited his parents that morning aboard the *River Queen*, which was serving as Lincoln's City Point headquarters, and he had reported, with the casualness of a seamy-faced veteran, that there had been "a little rumpus up the line."

That afternoon, while a truce was in effect at Fort Stedman so that the dead and wounded could be attended to, Federal troops of II and VI Corps probed the Confederate right to see if it had been weakened to provide men for the attack on Stedman. As early as 6 a.m., Major General Henry J. Hunt, the army's chief of artillery, had sent telegrams to the Federal corps commanders along the line, alerting them to the Confederate assault. Two of them, Major Generals Horatio G. Wright and Humphreys, felt that Lee must have had to seriously deplete his front lines to make his initial assault. Quickly marshaling their divisions — with Meade's approval — the generals advanced, easily taking the Confederate picket lines.

As the Federals dug in along their new front late in the day, Lee ordered counterattacks. A II Corps officer, Lieutenant Colonel Charles H. Weygant of the 124th New York, reported, "About 7 p.m. the pickets in our immediate front were driven in, closely followed by a force of the enemy. I allowed them to advance to within about eighty yards of the temporary line of works, behind which our men were concealed, when we poured a volley into them, driving them back about 100 yards to the picket-pits, where they rallied and made a stand. Cautioning the men to fire low, our fire soon became so effective as to almost silence the enemy, and caused them to crouch into the pits. I ordered a charge. The regiment rushed forward in a gallant style, capturing the battle flag of the Fifty Ninth Alabama. The enemy being completely dispersed, I returned to my former position." Most of the other counterattacks also were turned back, and at dusk the Federals held long sections of the Confederate rifle pits.

It was while this brisk fighting was taking place on the left that General Meade, who had returned to the front lines, took Lincoln to a hilltop fort from which a part of the battle was visible. The President cast his eye over the field, where Federal troops could be seen driving the enemy back, and commented, "This is better than a review." Lincoln also saw some of the wounded from the fighting at Fort Stedman; he said little, but a member of the party noted that he looked "worn and haggard." Later, Lincoln remarked quietly that he had seen enough of the horrors of war and hoped they would soon be concluded.

The day's events contributed to that end. The Battle of Fort Stedman was a major Federal victory. It was clear afterward that Lee could mount no more attacks on such a scale without risking the destruction of his army.

Meanwhile, critical events were occurring elsewhere. After his visit to Fort Stedman, Lincoln took the military railroad back to the *River Queen*. There, the following day, he would entertain a new visitor: General Sherman, who had come to report on a momentous two months in the Carolinas.

Standoff on the James

As Grant's army tightened its grip on Lee's forces at Petersburg early in 1865, a confrontation of a different kind was unfolding on the inland waters of Virginia. Just off City Point, the huge Federal supply base at the confluence of the James and Appomattox Rivers, Union gunboats detached from the North Atlantic Blockading Squadron patrolled nervously. A few miles to the north lay a formidable squadron of Confederate warships, including three powerful ironclads and seven gunboats, spoiling for a chance to steam downriver and strike.

It was the mission of the Federal flotilla to create an inland blockade to prevent the Confederates from dropping below City Point, where they could snap Grant's critical life line to the North. Though a showdown between the two fleets never occurred, they sparred menacingly through the last days of the War, with — in Grant's judgment — the survival of his army at stake.

Smokestacks and sidewheels protrude from the James River below Drewry's Bluff, where Confederates had deliberately sunk their own vessels to block the passage of Federal warships. Such obstructions were made even more treacherous by the addition of electrical mines that could be detonated from shore.

The *U.S.S. Commodore Morris* (*above*), a side-wheel ferryboat fitted with guns in 1862, spent its entire Civil War service patrolling the rivers and creeks of Virginia. The *Morris* was a multipurpose craft; in addition to attacking Confederate shore installations and ships, she transported troops and supplies and towed disabled vessels.

The James River, navigable for 80 miles — as far upstream as Richmond — was the scene of naval operations during the final campaigns of the War. Federal warships were prevented from attacking the Confederate capital by obstructions, by batteries at Drewry's Bluff and by ironclads of the Confederate Navy.

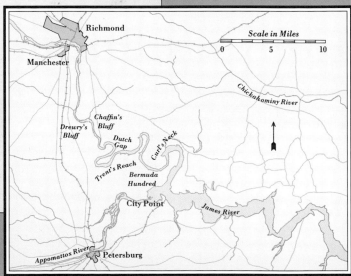

Federal monitors lining the river at Trent's Reach, near Dutch Gap, are led by the U.S.S. *Saugus* (above, foreground), which would serve as a temporary prison for the conspirators in Lincoln's assassination. Protruding from the bow of the *Saugus* is a torpedo rake, designed to catch and detonate mines before they came in contact with the ship's hull.

Crew members of the monitor *Sangamon* savor fresh air on the foredeck while a longboat prepares to ferry men ashore. The portable bellows and forge in the foreground were used for making repairs to the fittings of the ironclad vessel.

The Formidable Ironclads

Most of the responsibility for defending Grant's supply route against waterborne attacks fell to the class of vessels known as monitors. The shallow draft of these ships made them ideal for navigating the shoals and tricky currents of the James River close to Richmond; and the twin guns that were concealed within each monitor's revolving turret constituted a serious threat to Confederate forces afloat and ashore. "These boats," wrote Rear Admiral David D. Porter when a Confederate assault seemed imminent, "must be ready at all times, with steam up, to attack anything they are ordered to, and, when the opportunity occurs, the captains must not hesitate to sacrifice their boats if necessary."

A schooner delivering supplies contrasts with the lean lines and low freeboard of the steam-powered monitor *Canonicus*, named for a Narragansett Indian chief. The crew of the *Canonicus* took pride in the fact that the ironclad's flag was twice shot away and gallantly replaced under fire.

The powerful double-turreted *Onondaga*, flagship of the James River flotilla, lies at anchor near City Point. In January 1865, the *Onondaga*, supported by two gunboats, faced a threatened assault by the entire Confederate fleet. The attack stalled after three Confederate craft ran aground.

Gunboats Vulnerable to Ambush

The waters off City Point were patrolled not only by monitors but also by converted civilian boats of varying armament and seaworthiness. Most, like the *Mendota (below)*, were side-wheelers laden with guns. They escorted supply schooners and troop carriers from the Chesapeake Bay, guarding against Confederate raiders lurking onshore.

But the gunboats' decks left the crews vulnerable to sniper fire from the riverbanks. "We never knew," wrote one Navy officer, "when a distant crack and puff of smoke might claim another life."

Officers and crew gathered on the foredeck of the *Mendota* appear crisp and hardy despite the travail of long service on the gunboat. Cramped quarters and the oppressive, swamplike climate on the James made the sailors' lives miserable, and the ship had earlier been swept by an epidemic of malaria.

The U.S.S. *Mendota*, a double-ended gunboat capable of maneuvering in opposing directions without turning around, steams cautiously along the banks of the James, alert for Confederate batteries concealed in the brush. In addition to her complicated arrangement of twin rudders and wheelhouses, the *Mendota*, like many Federal steam vessels, had auxiliary masts for sailing.

An Armada of Expendables

While monitors and gunboats provided most of the firepower for the Federal force on the James River, a diverse collection of auxiliary vessels added sorely needed bulk to the inland blockade. Since many of the river's tributaries could be navigated only by shallow-draft vessels, dozens of steam-powered tugs, wooden schooners and even rowboats were put to use. So great was the need for small craft that captains of monitors and gunboats were forced to give up their whaleboats and personal launches.

Few of these expendable vessels had been built specifically for the military; therefore, their function depended largely on need — and on the ingenuity of their officers and men. Most often they convoyed supplies and war matériel, but on occasion they were pressed into service as scouts and mine sweepers. One enterprising crew, hoping to surprise and sink an unwary Confederate ironclad, rigged out their wooden rowboat with a 20-foot-long torpedo spar — despite the great risk to themselves.

The tugboat *Linda,* prosaically renamed torpedo tug No. 4, lands a detachment at Drewry's Bluff while other crew members lounge in the bow near the tug's torpedo boom. The boom was tipped with a 150-pound spar torpedo, which could be lowered into the water and run alongside an enemy ship. The charge would then be detonated by a lanyard.

Armed with cutlasses and rifles, a landing party comes ashore to flush out Confederate sharpshooters. Roving Confederate scouts were active along the banks of the James both above and below City Point, keeping the Union fleet always on the alert.

The 512-ton gunboat *Commodore Perry (left)*, a converted ferryboat, was in action almost every day of the campaign, pummeling Confederate shore positions with its Parrot guns and 32-pounder smoothbores. In one notable two-hour artillery duel, the *Commodore Perry* sustained six hits and expended all of its ammunition before driving off the Confederates.

49

Members of the crew of the U.S.S. *Mendota* muster on the foredeck near one of their two 100-pounder Parrot guns. The *Mendota* also boasted eight smaller artillery pieces, making her one of the most powerful ships on the river. Hanging over the ship's rail are heavy nets, intended to thwart Confederate boarding parties.

An armada of Federal warships maintains its vigil on the Appomattox River near City Point. As late as April of 1865, as the ground combat swept westward, General Grant requested additional gunboats to patrol the James and the Appomattox, lest the Confederate squadron "attempt to come to City Point during the absence of the greater part of the army."

Vengeance in the Carolinas

Of the 11 Confederate states, the one most fervently detested in the North — and whose occupation was most eagerly anticipated by Federal soldiers as 1864 ended — was South Carolina, birthplace of secession and site of the War's opening hostilities. South Carolinians, the firebrands of the Confederacy, were held responsible for the conflict and for all its disasters and discomforts. General Sherman's troops — and their commander — could scarcely wait to exact retribution.

"The truth is," Sherman wrote on Christmas Eve to Major General Henry W. Halleck, the chief of staff in Washington, "the whole army is burning with an insatiable desire to wreak vengeance upon South Carolina. I almost tremble at her fate, but feel that she deserves all that seems in store for her."

Even on their recently completed march through Georgia to Savannah, Federal soldiers had shown a certain objectivity toward their enemy: They inflicted a great deal of damage but acted for the most part without evidence of malice. A march through South Carolina would be different. "I want to see the long-deferred chastisement begin," an Illinois soldier wrote home. "If we don't purify South Carolina, it will be because we can't get a light."

For a time in December, however, it looked as though the punishment would not be meted out after all. Ulysses S. Grant had reluctantly decided against sending Sherman north by land. Heavy winter rains customar-ily turned the state's myriad streams into rushing torrents, the lowlands into swamps and the roads into sloughs.

But Sherman was used to doing the impossible, and he continued to urge that the invasion be launched. The weather did not concern him, he said. As a young lieutenant he had spent four years in Charleston, and he knew all about the winters there. What was more, his men were champing to go. "I never saw a more confident army," Sherman wrote to his wife. "The soldiers think I know everything and that they can do anything."

Grant soon relented, in part because he had discovered that his alternative plan — transporting Sherman's army to Virginia by steamer — would take two months to execute. It would be better after all, Grant decided, to strike into the Carolinas, "to disorganize the South, and prevent the organization of new armies from their broken fragments."

Grant began making massive preparations to ensure Sherman's success. A division from XIX Corps was sent by sea to garrison Savannah, so that Sherman could take all of his veterans with him. Major General John M. Schofield's XXIII Corps was detached from the Army of the Cumberland — which had just administered a smashing defeat at Nashville to General John Bell Hood and the Confederate Army of Tennessee. Schofield's new assignment was to occupy the North Carolina port of Wilmington, then move in-

A torch fashioned by a Union soldier from kindling wood, rope and hemp survived the burning of Columbia, the capital of South Carolina, during its occupation by Sherman's vengeful XV Corps. "Now that we were in South Carolina, the leading State in bringing on this War," wrote a soldier from Ohio, "I felt the people were entitled to share its hardships."

land to Goldsboro, which was roughly halfway between Savannah and Richmond. After repairing the railroad to Goldsboro and establishing a supply base there for Federal forces, he and his more than 20,000 men would join Sherman for the push through North Carolina and into Virginia.

As Sherman prepared to march, General P.G.T. Beauregard, head of the Military Division of the West, tried urgently to scrape together an army that could stop him. The nearest Confederate force north of Savannah comprised 8,000 men under Lieutenant General William J. Hardee at Port Royal Sound, South Carolina. Hardee also had a 3,000-man division of state militia defending Charleston. Farther up the coast, General Braxton Bragg, recently dispatched from Richmond, commanded a force of about 6,500 at Wilmington. Major General Daniel Harvey Hill, headquartered at Augusta, blocked Sherman's inland route with three divisions of Major General Joseph Wheeler's roving cavalry and about 1,400 Georgia militia, who were prohibited by law from leaving their home state.

Beauregard hoped to augment this inadequate force with troops from the Army of Tennessee, which was licking its wounds at Tupelo, Mississippi. Of the 40,000 tough veterans that Hood had led into battle at Nashville, fewer than half remained. Hood himself, broken in spirit, had been relieved of command at his own request. Still, this was the most potent Confederate force in the field other than the Army of Northern Virginia, and 11,000 of its men were ordered east by rail to Augusta. In addition, Robert E. Lee reluctantly parted with the redoubtable Wade Hampton — now promoted to

lieutenant general — sending him to his native South Carolina with a division of his cavalry under Major General Matthew C. Butler. Even if Beauregard could assemble every available soldier in the region, however, he would have fewer than 30,000 men. Sherman, once Schofield's force joined him, would command more than 70,000.

As Sherman was about to move north from Savannah in mid-January of 1865, the rains arrived. The area was inundated, and there were days when even Sherman wondered if the pessimists had been right about his chances of making a winter march through the Carolinas. Sherman's plan was to keep the enemy confused about where he was headed. As they did through Georgia, his troops would march in two columns. His left wing — the XIV and XX Corps, led by the hard-bitten Major General Henry W. Slocum — would travel northwest to threaten Augusta. The devout but soldierly Major General Oliver O. Howard would take the right wing, consisting of XV Corps and XVII Corps, northeast toward Charleston. But the Federals' real objective was Columbia, the capital of South Carolina, 130 miles due north of Savannah.

The downpour that coincided with Sherman's planned departure was the heaviest in 20 years, and the roads on the South Carolina side of the Savannah River — the first of several major rivers to be crossed between Savannah and Goldsboro — were said to be "navigable in boats."

For a full 10 days, the left wing was stopped in its tracks. The experience of one regiment, the 123rd New York, was typical. First, its soldiers had to move their camp back from the rising river to avoid being drowned. Then, on January 28, the men marched several miles to a river crossing, found the bridge washed out, returned to camp, went back and attempted to make a new bridge, had to give up and camped again not far from where they had begun.

The next day the New Yorkers tried a different crossing — a causeway that ran across a swamp, with a bridged creek cutting through it. They fought off a brief attack by Confederate cavalry, then went on to examine the causeway. "We found it covered with water in many places," recalled Sergeant Rice Bull, "and in some low places it was two or more feet deep. The only guide we had over the flooded road were the posts and railing on each side of the causeway. Upon reaching the creek we found the bridge all

gone." The men were thereupon ordered back to their starting point. It was the 5th of February before the left wing finally got across the Savannah.

Before the rains came, most of the right wing's XVII Corps, under Major General Francis P. Blair Jr., had moved by ship 30 miles up the coast to Beaufort, South Carolina. Major General John A. Logan's XV Corps followed by land and sea, and at the end of January, Howard's wing reassembled near Pocotaligo, a village 35 miles inland. The wing moved out on the 1st of February through drenched terrain, criss-crossed with streams, that had become one continuous swamp — "Frog Heaven," the soldiers called it. Sherman compared the swamp to a Fourth of July political oration: "only knee

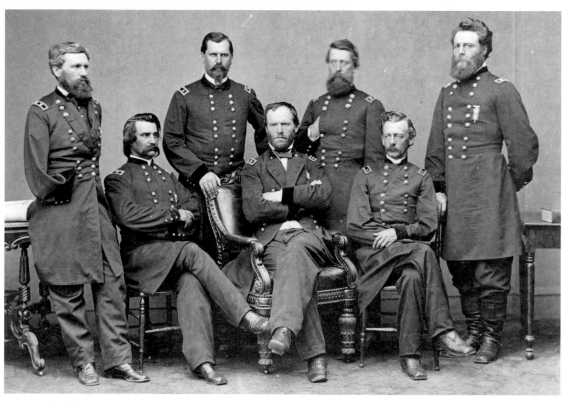

OLIVER O. HOWARD   WILLIAM B. HAZEN   JEFFERSON C. DAVIS   JOSEPH A. MOWER

JOHN A. LOGAN   WILLIAM T. SHERMAN   HENRY W. SLOCUM

William Tecumseh Sherman, seated at center, is joined by six of the generals who served under him through the march to the sea and the Carolinas campaigns. After weeding out those commanders he considered unfit, Sherman praised his remaining subordinates for honing his army's "tone and temper" and for their "cheerfulness and harmony of action."

deep, but spread out over all creation." In fact, the water was chest deep — and Sherman's men often had to wade through it for miles. They made no effort to be quiet, but called out warnings and imprecations to one another as they struggled to extricate draft animals from the ooze. To add to the din, one regimental commander issued a whiskey ration to his grateful men "in view of the exposure." As a result, said one soldier, "such a wild scene of splashing and yelling and braying has rarely greeted mortal eyes and ears." Confederate snipers were all about, and the Federal skirmishers watched each other closely; a wounded man would drown unless help reached him quickly.

Sherman could not count on receiving regular supplies until he reached a new base, so he was traveling with an unusually large number of wagons — about 2,500. Since he dared not leave wounded men behind in hostile country, he had also brought 600 ambulances. The wagons and ambulances, added to the army's 68 guns, made up a train 25 miles long that churned the mud of the roads into a deep, heavy broth.

Captain George Ward Nichols, Sherman's aide-de-camp, described what often happened: "A wagon, painfully toiling along the road, suddenly careens; the wheels are submerged in a quicksand; every effort of the mules or horses to pull out only buries the unfortunate vehicle deeper in the mire, and very soon the animals have dug for themselves a pit, out of which many are never extricated alive."

One or two wagons stuck in this way, Nichols observed, "showed at once that the road must be corduroyed." Corduroying, a soldier wrote, was "detestable work." Logs had to be cut from the surrounding forests, trimmed, flattened on one side, and laid across the road to provide a solid surface for the animals and wagons. Saplings were then fitted between the logs. The men who had been chosen to serve as pioneers struggled for hours in the rain, knee-deep in the swamp. Corduroying was not only arduous; it could be dangerous. One campaigner noted in his diary that in a single day two men in his unit were killed by falling trees and a third "tried to lose an axe in his foot."

The speed of the Federal advance under these daunting circumstances stunned the Confederates. "I wouldn't have believed it if I hadn't seen it happen," General Hardee said later. And perhaps the ultimate accolade was delivered by a Confederate prisoner. If Sherman's men were sent to hell, he commented sourly to one of his captors, "they'd corduroy it and march on."

The hamlets in the southern part of South Carolina were the first to feel the fury of Sherman's invasion. Hardeeville, just across the Savannah, was burned to the ground. It could not have been a very handsome place to begin with, remarked Sergeant Bull of the 123rd New York, but "now it can hardly be described, because there was not much of it left standing."

Bull's account of his regiment's passage through the southern part of the state is a litany of destruction. On February 4, he camped on the grounds of a fine plantation; the mansion house was still standing, but "completely wrecked." The next day he entered the village of Robertsville, "now consisting chiefly of chimneys and ash heaps." A resident of Robertsville, returning after the Union soldiers had passed through, found "but one fence paling to indicate the site of our little village."

Holding their muskets and cartridge boxes high, Federal infantrymen — identified by their tattered national colors as part of the Army of the Tennessee — slog through a South Carolina swamp. After wading for an hour across such a swamp, one Union soldier muttered to a comrade, "I think we've struck this river lengthways!"

On February 5, Sherman's aggressive cavalry commander, Brigadier General Hugh Judson Kilpatrick, had struck Barnwell, a prosperous community of 400 that boasted several churches and public buildings, a women's seminary and a Masonic lodge. All were torched. Kilpatrick never denied the rumor circulating in the army that he had filled his men's saddlebags with matches in preparation for the campaign.

Mrs. Alfred P. Aldrich, mistress of a nearby plantation, later described the arrival of the Federal cavalrymen. They came "pouring in at every door," she said, and began ripping the locks from bureaus and wardrobes as they sought gold, silver and jewels. "Finding nothing to satisfy their cupidity

thus far, they began turning over mattresses, tearing open feather beds, and scattering the contents in the wildest confusion." Then they discovered some whiskey. The liquor, she said, "seemed to infuriate and rouse all their evil passions, so that the work of destruction began in earnest." Tables were knocked over, lamps and the kerosene inside them were "thrown over carpets and mattings, furniture of all sorts broken, a guitar and violin smashed."

Mrs. Aldrich managed to save her home from complete ruin, but the residents of Barnwell were less fortunate. "All the public buildings were destroyed," she wrote. "The fine brick courthouse, with most of the stores, laid level with the ground, and many

General Zachariah Deas (*inset*), resisting Sherman's advance toward Columbia, had orders to demolish any bridge he could not hold. But the razing of Shilling's Bridge over the Edisto River (*below*) slowed the Federals only briefly; at left, skirmishers of XV Corps ford the stream while the first men across clear the woods of lingering Confederates.

private residences, with only the chimneys standing like grim sentinels; the Masonic Hall in ashes." The Federal soldiers grinned as they marched away and told each other that now the town would have to change its name from Barnwell to Burnwell.

In the first three weeks of the march northward, a dozen communities were ransacked and razed. Even the countryside, remote from Sherman's route, was not immune to the vandalism. Much of the damage was inflicted by Sherman's foragers. At first, as he had in the Georgia Campaign, Sherman tried to control the foraging in the Carolinas. Each brigade sent out parties under the command of an officer to demand supplies from civilians and to distribute them through reg-

ular channels. But the task was monumental. As an Illinois private explained, "We were told in no uncertain terms that henceforth we must live off the country or go hungry. We did both."

Regiments began to fend for themselves, dispatching men each morning to scour the countryside and return that night with food. Virtually every man in the army pulled foraging duty at one time or another, but a certain type of individual gravitated to the work, volunteered for it — and excelled at it. These were men of unusual independence and inventiveness who chafed under the discipline of the march. Some, more renegades than soldiers, adopted a shabby style of their own, shunning uniforms for outlandish costumes stolen from their victims. They were hard men, untroubled by the desperate plight of the civilians upon whom they preyed. The soldiers called these scavengers "bummers," a name that once meant any man who shirked ordinary duties, and regarded their exploits with amusement, if not a touch of envy.

Others were less approving. "Think how you would admire him," wrote a reporter for the New York *Herald,* "if you were a lone woman, with a family of five children, far from help, when he blandly inquired where you kept your valuables. Think how you would smile when he pried open your chests with his bayonet, or knocked to pieces your tables, pianos and chairs." Many of these marauders, the correspondent said, "are loaded down with silver-ware, gold coin, and other valuables. I hazard nothing in saying three-fifths (in value) of the personal property of the counties we have passed through were taken by Sherman's army."

Despite the concern expressed by several of his officers, Sherman was well satisfied with the performance of his foragers. "They are organized for a very useful purpose from the adventurous spirits who are always found in the ranks," he said, "and are indispensable in feeding troops when compelled, like my army, to live off the country."

Because they were so effective—and even more because of their notorious behavior—the foragers became prime targets for the Confederate cavalry. And they were highly vulnerable, since they traveled in small, more or less defenseless groups. Robert H. Strong, an infantryman in the 105th Illinois, told of a party of foragers separated from his regiment by the sudden flooding of a rain-swollen river. The next day, some soldiers

from the regiment got across the river and found two of the foragers hanging from a tree. "Their throats were cut," said Strong, "and pinned to their drawers was a piece of paper with the words 'Death to all foragers' written on it."

The Confederates were scarcely in a position to criticize the conduct of the enemy. For at least nine months, Wheeler's cavalrymen had been living entirely on what they could wrest from the countryside, and some Southerners considered them worse marauders than the Yankees. The most visible—and the most widely reported—abuse by Wheeler's men occurred as the Federal army reached its initial objective.

Columbia, South Carolina, was an elegant city. "The private residences," said Captain Nichols, "are large and roomy, and are surrounded with gardens which, even at this wintry season of the year, are filled with hedges, flowering shrubs and bordered walks, all in summer green." The city was terribly overcrowded, however. No one in the South had expected the War to reach Columbia, and it had become a haven for refugees. In two years its population had swollen from 8,000 to about 20,000. Columbia was a significant railroad and manufacturing center, and Sherman considered it a vital target. His soldiers concurred: "Hail, Columbia, happy land," they sang as they marched, "If I don't burn you, I'll be damned!"

Wheeler's men had ridden into Columbia on February 16, purportedly to defend the city. Instead, according to a Southern reporter, they "proceeded to break into the stores along main street and rob them of their contents," apparently rationalizing their behavior with the assumption that the Union soldiers would soon be along to steal the goods anyway. Then, after skirmishing briefly with the advancing Federals, the Confederate horsemen rode away, many of them laden with plunder.

The Federals arrived the next morning. One of the first units to enter the city was an all-Iowa brigade of XV Corps, led by Colonel George A. Stone. The Iowans, who were to serve as provost guards, had marched for 24 hours and were exhausted, hungry — and thirsty. "Some foolish persons, thinking to please the soldiers, brought out whiskey by the pailfuls," wrote one officer, "and before the superior officers were aware of it, a good many of Stone's brigade were intoxicated." The liquor was passed along the ranks of the marchers; in one instance a large tin boiler was used. The unit was quickly relieved, and the drunken men were put under arrest.

But more whiskey was available. By nightfall, said John Logan, the corps commander, "the citizens had so crazed our men with liquor that it was impossible to control them." The result was predictable, as General Slocum observed: "A drunken soldier with a musket in one hand and a match in the other is not a pleasant visitor to have about the house on a dark, windy night." Fires started. Some men fought them. Others fed them. "By the red glare," wrote Emma LeConte, a 17-year-old Columbia girl, "we could watch the wretches walking — generally staggering — back and forth from camp to the town — shouting — hurrahing — cursing South Carolina — swearing — blaspheming — singing ribald songs and using such obscene language that we were forced to go indoors."

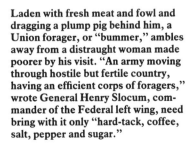

Laden with fresh meat and fowl and dragging a plump pig behind him, a Union forager, or "bummer," ambles away from a distraught woman made poorer by his visit. "An army moving through hostile but fertile country, having an efficient corps of foragers," wrote General Henry Slocum, commander of the Federal left wing, need bring with it only "hard-tack, coffee, salt, pepper and sugar."

Strong winds sweep streamers of flame and debris across the night sky above reveling Federals in Columbia, South Carolina, on February 17, 1865. Columbia's Mayor, Thomas J. Goodwyn (*above*), had met that morning with Sherman and received assurance that the citizens and their property would not be harmed — a promise that was not kept.

According to Sergeant Theodore F. Upson of the 100th Indiana, one reeling soldier attired in a dressing gown separated himself from the mob and presented himself to Sherman. Raising his newly acquired plug hat, he said to his grinning commander: "I have the honor (hic), General, to present (hic) you with (hic) the freedom of the (hic) city." A guard grabbed the man and hustled him off.

The origins of the fires in Columbia that night later became a subject of controversy. Wade Hampton contended that Sherman, after promising city officials that Columbia would be saved, had "burned the city to the ground, deliberately, systematically and atrociously." Sherman claimed the fires already were burning when his men arrived and that Hampton himself must accept responsibility for them. Confederate cavalry, he maintained, had set fire to bales of cotton

so the Federals would not get them, and the high wind had then spread the flames across the city. It was a meaningless dispute: Certainly the Federal soldiers did not prevent the blaze from consuming Columbia. Sherman later said as much. "Though I never ordered it and never wished it," he declared, "I have never shed any tears over the event, because I believe that it hastened what we all fought for, the end of the War."

Captain Orlando M. Poe, Sherman's chief engineer, had seen much of war, but the conflagration in Columbia appalled him. "The burning houses, lighting up the faces of shrieking women, terrified children and frantic, raving, drunken men, formed a scene which no man of the slightest sensibility wants to witness a second time," wrote Poe in his official report.

Belatedly, the Federal authorities took

One resident of Columbia, Lucy Green, hid her valuables in these pouches when she and her family left the imperiled city. Emma LeConte, another young woman who was preparing to flee, wrote in her journal on February 15: "I have been hastily making large pockets to wear under my hoopskirt, for they will hardly search our persons."

steps to recover control of the situation. A brigade swept through the city with instructions to arrest all disorderly persons. Sherman sent bucket brigades to the rooftops. Early the following morning, the wind subsided and the spread of the fire was halted. For a time, shadowy figures could be seen running through the streets carrying torches or buckets of turpentine, but the provost guards shot several of these would-be arsonists and drove the rest from the streets.

Columbia was in ruins. Nothing could be seen, said Emma LeConte, but "heaps of rubbish, tall dreary chimneys, and shattered brick walls." By one count, 458 buildings had burned, and thousands of the city's inhabitants — mostly women and children — were without shelter. "Two-thirds of the city," said Mayor Thomas J. Goodwyn, "is in ashes." In the two days that followed, Sherman's men added to the rubble by destroying warehouses, public buildings and railroad properties — any remaining structures of potential use to the Confederacy.

On February 17, the day Columbia fell, the Confederates had evacuated Charleston, about 100 miles to the southeast. Union forces occupied central South Carolina and were threatening Wilmington; as a result, Charleston was cut off and could not be held.

The Confederates' opposition to Sherman's drive remained virtually nonexistent. Wheeler's cavalry had not made much of an impression on Sherman's host; Bragg's forces did little to interfere with Schofield's occupation of Wilmington on the 22nd; Hardee had lingered helplessly in Charleston; and the Army of Tennessee was still laboriously making its way east over the Confederacy's rickety railroads. Beauregard, ailing and uncertain, was falling back with his troops toward North Carolina.

General Lee and the Confederate Congress insisted that Joseph Johnston, who had been replaced by Hood the previous July, be reinstated as chief of the Army of Tennessee and subsequently as commander of all the troops opposing Sherman. Johnston accepted the assignment reluctantly on February 23: "It is too late," he told an aide. Nevertheless, he set about pulling his scattered forces together. The army greeted the news of his return with pleasure. "Thank God he has been reinstated," an army inspector said in a letter home. Johnston, he felt, would impose discipline on the army which was "now a complete mob."

Worse, it was a shrinking mob. Many of its soldiers were Georgians, and their route east that month had taken them across the path of Sherman's march to the sea. Deeply concerned about their families, they had deserted by the hundreds. "Who can blame them for doing so?" asked one of their officers. Many of the men later returned to their commands, but only 4,000 of the expected 11,000 troops reached North Carolina.

Meanwhile, Sherman had resumed his drive, striking northeast toward Goldsboro. His progress was slowed not by the enemy, but by a new hindrance. All through South Carolina, slaves seeking liberation had attached themselves to the Federal columns, as they had in Georgia. By the time Sherman's army entered North Carolina in the first week of March, the refugees numbered in the thousands — "at times," said General Slocum, "they were almost equal in numbers

Scenes of Ruin in Columbia

General Sherman noted blandly in his memoirs that on February 20, 1865, the right wing of his army resumed its northward march "having utterly ruined Columbia." Richard Wearn, a local photographer, was himself ruined, having lost his gallery to the fires that swept through the South Carolina capital during the Federal occupation. Undaunted, Wearn loaded his cameras in a wagon and toured his city, photographing the wreckage and in one instance (below, left) including himself in the picture.

Wearn recorded a landscape of stark destruction. Columbia's venerable Statehouse, with its law library and archives, had burned to the ground, although a half-built new Statehouse (below, right and bottom right) came through almost unscathed. Another extensive library was lost when fire gutted the home of Dr. Robert W. Gibbes, South Carolina's Surgeon General (opposite, middle left). Also destroyed were the city's best hotel (opposite, top right), six churches, 11 banks and a printing plant (opposite, bottom right) where Confederate currency was printed.

To some, the most poignant loss was the Ursuline Convent and Academy (opposite, bottom left), where the daughters of prominent families, Northern and Southern, had been educated. The convent's mother superior had taught Sherman's daughter, Minnie, in Ohio before the War, but her school was not spared.

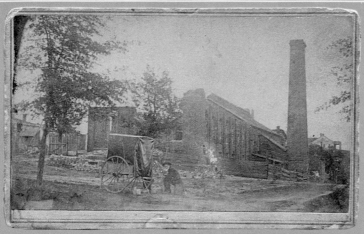

PHOTOGRAPHER RICHARD WEARN IN FRONT OF THE STATE ARMORY

MAIN STREET, LOOKING NORTH TOWARD THE NEW STATEHOUSE

MAIN STREET, LOOKING SOUTH FROM THE STATEHOUSE GROUNDS

SOUTH FAÇADE OF THE NEW STATEHOUSE, FROM MAIN STREET

FREIGHT DEPOT OF THE SOUTH CAROLINA RAILROAD

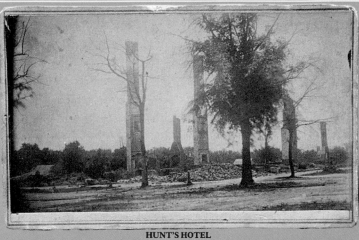

HUNT'S HOTEL

HOME OF DR. ROBERT W. GIBBES, STATE SURGEON GENERAL

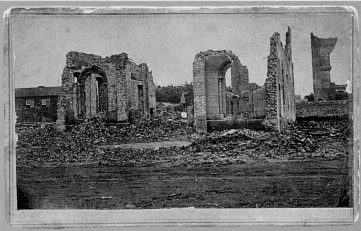

DISTRICT JAIL

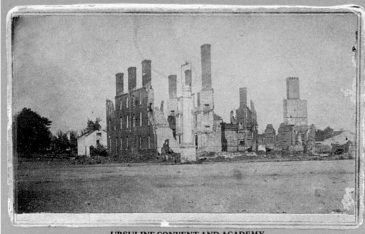

URSULINE CONVENT AND ACADEMY

EVANS & COGSWELL, CONFEDERATE GOVERNMENT PRINTERS

to the army they were following.'' Although many of the blacks could forage for themselves, Sherman complained that they ''have clung to our skirts, impeded our movements and consumed our food.''

The three Federal columns converging on Goldsboro — Sherman's forces from Columbia and Schofield's XXIII Corps from Wilmington — were, despite their combined numerical advantage, vulnerable to separate attack. Sherman knew it, and he was trying to keep the two wings of his main army from drifting too far apart. By early March much

of Schofield's corps had not yet reached New Bern, 50 miles east of Goldsboro.

The Confederates were watching closely. Johnston, concentrating his forces at Smithfield, North Carolina, 30 miles northwest of Goldsboro, did not yet have enough troops to attack the main Federal columns. But Bragg, on his way from Wilmington with Major General Robert Hoke's division to join Johnston, thought he saw a chance to strike a decisive blow. Schofield's troops, he reported to Johnston on March 6, were nearing the town of Kinston, ''in heavy force and mov-

The 55th Massachusetts, a black infantry regiment, receives a jubilant welcome from blacks lining the streets of Charleston on February 21, 1865, three days after Confederate forces and most of the white citizens abandoned the shell-damaged port. ''Cheers, blessings, prayers were heard on every side,'' wrote Lieutenant Colonel Charles B. Fox, the regiment's white commanding officer.

ing in confidence. A few hours would suffice to unite the forces at Smithfield with mine and ensure a victory." Johnston sent D. H. Hill at once, with part of the newly arrived Army of Tennessee, to join Bragg.

The Federal force that Bragg had reported sighting was a provisional corps of 13,000 men under Major General Jacob D. Cox, which had been standing guard while the railroad between New Bern and Goldsboro was being repaired to function as Sherman's supply line. On March 7, the Federals encountered Bragg at Southwest Creek, a wide stream that flowed into the Neuse River at a point three miles east of Kinston. Control of the creek and the roads that crossed it, including the railroad, was the key to controlling troop and supply movements in the area, and it was here that Bragg hoped to stop — or at least delay — Cox's westward advance. He entrenched his 6,000 troops along the west bank of the creek, directly in Cox's path.

Cox saw at once that Southwest Creek and its crossings were worth fighting for. He wrote later that "the slight ridge on the hither side of that stream was the only dry land in the vicinity, and upon it were the principal roads." He moved his troops to the edge of the swampland east of the river. Brigadier General Innis Palmer's division, on the right, protected the railroad. About a mile south of Palmer, Brigadier General Samuel Carter's division covered the Dover road, a major route through the spongy terrain between New Bern and Kinston. The 12th New York Cavalry patrolled the roads to the left. A mile in front of the Federal position, an old track known as the British road ran parallel to Southwest Creek. Where it crossed the Dover road, Colonel Charles Upham of Carter's division was stationed with two regiments, the 15th Connecticut and the 27th Massachusetts. A reserve division, made up of green troops led by Brigadier General Thomas Ruger, assumed a position at Gum Swamp, at the end of the unfinished rail line and about three miles behind Carter and Palmer.

When Cox discovered that the bridges for the railroad and the Dover road, as well as for the Neuse road, to the north, had been destroyed, he ordered his men to search along the creek for a place across which a footbridge could be constructed. General Schofield was expected that evening at Gum Swamp, and Cox, after leaving instructions, rode off to meet his superior's train.

Before dawn on the 8th of March, D. H. Hill arrived with 2,000 men, a mixed group comprising veterans of the Army of Tennessee and youthful members of the North Carolina Junior Reserves. Their coming boosted the size of Bragg's force to roughly 8,000 men. A few hours later the Confederates advanced; Hoke crossed the creek and headed north on the British road, unmolested by Federal cavalry. When Upham heard that Confederate troops were moving on his left, he placed the 27th Massachusetts across the British road about 500 yards beyond the Dover road, facing southwest. At noon, Hoke crashed into the New Englanders' eastern flank.

The 27th had lost several hundred men the previous May at Drewry's Bluff and had been built back to strength with recruits who were no match for Hoke's seasoned troops. At one point Colonel Upham called for artillery support; a battery came up, he said, "but passed on the run under a very hot musketry fire, and I have not seen the officer in command of it since." After a brief struggle, the regiment was captured nearly intact.

At the sound of the fighting, D. H. Hill crossed Southwest Creek and attempted to turn the Federal right. His Junior Reserves "advanced very handsomely for a time," Hill reported, but then one regiment broke for the rear and "the rest lay down and could not be got forward." Hill left them behind, advanced with the rest of his men and cornered Upham's other regiment, the 15th Connecticut. "This movement was completely successful," he wrote later, "and the Yankees ran in the wildest confusion."

A rout was in the making. "I had nothing to do now," Hill reported, "but press forward rapidly to the firing and intercept the foe fleeing from Hoke. I think that with little loss we would have captured several thousand men." But as Hill was preparing to deliver the blow, he got orders from Bragg to move his forces five miles north to the intersection of the British and Neuse roads; there, Bragg said, Hill "would make many captures." Hill complied, but he found no Federals in the new place and eventually was ordered back to his original position. By the time he returned, the opportunity had been lost. But some damage already had been done: The 15th Connecticut had been captured, almost en masse. A private who had missed the fighting wrote home, "I am obliged to tell that the brave Fifteenth are no more, they were nearly all taken prisoners. They were surrounded by a division of rebs and they fought bravely and were slaughtered at the onset." Upham had lost his two regiments, a total of 860 men, in a single day.

General Cox had returned to the Federal lines from the railhead at Gum Swamp after receiving word of Upham's predicament. He fortified his left with a brigade from Palmer's

IMPORTANT APPEAL.

Headquarters Division of the West,

CHARLOTTE, N. C., FEB. 23d, 1865.

To delay the advance of the enemy until our troops can be massed in strength sufficient to crush him, I appeal to all good and patriotic citizens in the region of country threatened by the enemy to turn out in full force all available labor with axes, spades and mattocks to destroy and obstruct roads leading towards Charlotte from the South—commencing first along the roads leading to Lands Ford and other crossings between that point and the Rail Road Bridge—obstructing at the same time all roads parallel to the river within the following limits: The Pleasant Valley Road on the East to a point opposite Lands Ford, thence across the Catawba to Fishing Creek; thence up said Creek to the Charlotte and South Carolina Rail Road. Afterwards the work should be continued further up the River should the enemy threaten an advance in that direction. The negroes should be assembled at the following points, viz:

Charlotte, Pleasant Valley, Bell Air, Lands Ford, Fort Mills, and Rock Hill, under the direction of their owners, each with six days' provisions, cooking utensils, and blankets. As far as possible the negroes will be employed at points not distant from their homes. They will be protected by guards and assisted by the Home Guards of the State.

An Engineer Officer will be at each of the points of rendezvous to give proper direction to the labor of all who will now join us in the struggle to stay and destroy the ruthless invaders of our homes.

G. T. BEAUREGARD,
GENERAL.

CHARLOTTE, FEB. 23d.

I earnestly appeal to the people of North Carolina to comply promptly with this request. I am satisfied they could render no greater service to their country.

Z. B. VANCE,
Governor of North Carolina.

Brandishing bowie knives and revolvers, brothers Daniel, John and Pleasant Chitwood link arms and glower at the camera after enlisting in the "Barstow County Yankee Killers," later designated Company A of the 23rd Georgia. Pleasant Chitwood died of dysentery in 1862, but Daniel and John soldiered on in Hardee's corps, resisting Sherman's advance through Georgia and the Carolinas.

division and moved Ruger into the gap between Carter and Palmer. Cox also fortified and extended his breastworks on the left. Fierce skirmishes continued through the next day, but the Confederates did not come again in force until about noon on March 10, when Hoke's men once more attacked the Federal left. This time, Carter's artillery and infantry fire drove off the Confederates in less than an hour. Hill struck at Ruger's position and was repulsed in a similar fashion. By now, Federal strength was mounting rapidly — the rest of Schofield's XXIII Corps was approaching from New Bern — so Bragg ordered a withdrawal. The Confederates crossed the Neuse River that evening and encamped near Kinston. The attack had cost Bragg 134 casualties; most of the 1,257 men Cox lost had been captured.

On March 11, Sherman, accompanying General Slocum and the left wing, arrived at Fayetteville, on the Cape Fear River roughly 75 miles upstream from Wilmington. It turned out to be a welcome stop because of what happened the following afternoon. Sherman related that his men heard in the distance "the shrill whistle of a steamboat, which came nearer and nearer, and soon a shout, long and continuous, was raised down by the river, which spread farther and farther, and we all felt that it meant a messenger from home." So it was. The steamer from Wilmington carried the first word the men had received from outside since leaving Savannah more than a month before.

Before leaving Fayetteville, Sherman gave special attention to the arsenal there. It was a former Federal installation that the Confederates had expanded and put to heavy use. "I cannot leave a detachment to hold it," Sher-

Confederate artillerymen under Major General Robert Hoke *(inset)*, a North Carolinian defending his home ground, fire across Southwest Creek at Jackson's Mill, near Kinston, on March 9. At left rear, Federal infantrymen counterattack across the hotly contested Atlantic & North Carolina Railroad.

man told Secretary of War Stanton, "therefore shall burn it, blow it up with gunpowder, and then with rams knock down its walls. I take it for granted the United States will never again trust North Carolina with an arsenal to appropriate at her pleasure."

Sherman knew that the Confederates would try to stop him somewhere, and as he moved into North Carolina he became increasingly wary. He had heard that Joseph Johnston, for whom he had great respect, was once again his adversary. And on March 15, a guest at Sherman's dinner table grudgingly confirmed that General Hardee's corps was close at hand and ready to fight.

The guest was one of Hardee's brigade commanders, Colonel Albert Rhett. While skirmishing with the Federal advance guard, Rhett had blundered into a unit of enemy cavalrymen, whom he mistook for Confederates. When the troopers ordered him to halt — as Sherman recounted it, "in language more forcible than polite" — Rhett had threatened to report them to General Hampton for insubordination. When his mistake was pointed out to him, he surrendered in disgust; a few hours later he found himself dining with Sherman.

General Johnston had no way of knowing whether Sherman's next move would be north to Raleigh or northeast to Goldsboro. The Confederate commander had been trying to concentrate his forces at Smithfield, midway between the two cities, in order to comply with Lee's suggestion that he attack one of Sherman's wings in an effort to defeat the larger army in detail. But Bragg had not yet reached Smithfield with his 8,000 men, and Johnston desperately needed more time. It was Hardee's assignment to get it for him.

Hardee had entrenched his small corps on a narrow ridge between the Cape Fear River and a swamp near the village of Averasboro, which Slocum's left wing would have to pass to get to either Raleigh or Goldsboro. There Hardee's 7,500 men stopped Judson Kilpatrick's cavalry screen on the day Rhett was captured. The next morning, Hardee resumed his attack on the Federal cavalry and by 10 a.m. he had nearly turned Kilpatrick's right flank when portions of the Federal XX Corps arrived. Three batteries were placed in a commanding position and began to pound the Confederate line. While two infantry brigades pressed Hardee's front, Sherman directed Colonel Henry Case's brigade to move north along a creek bed, past the Confederate right flank, and attack from the rear. "As soon as we got in behind them we started with a yell on the double quick," an Illinois private wrote to his parents. By coincidence, the brunt of the surprise attack fell on Rhett's brigade, a hodgepodge of garrison and artillery units fighting as infantry under a new commander, Colonel William Butler. They were no match for Case's veteran troops. "I was never so pleased in my life as I was to see the rebs get up and try to get out of the way," exulted the soldier from Illinois. "I tell you there was a good many of them bit the dust."

Panic spread along the Confederate works and the line fell back. It started as a rout—

the troops left behind their knapsacks, muskets and even swords—but somehow they managed to form another line several hundred yards to the rear. The 1st and 3rd Divisions of XX Corps, augmented by a brigade from XIV Corps, advanced on this second line while Kilpatrick moved on the right. Threatened with a flanking movement, Hardee withdrew his men to a third position a mile away, on rising ground behind a small swamp. There the determined Confederates withstood repeated Federal attacks throughout the afternoon, suffering 865 casualties and inflicting 682, until twilight brought an end to the day's fighting. Having done all he could, Hardee slipped away that night to Smithfield.

Once more Slocum's wing started north. The Federal columns were having trouble staying together in the rain and mud. "In spite of every exertion," wrote General Cox, "the columns were a good deal drawn out, and long intervals separated the divisions." Thus extended, the Federal troops would have difficulty fending off an attack, and it was at this critical juncture—when the Federals were halfway between Fayetteville and Goldsboro and due south of Smithfield— that Johnston prepared to strike.

Although Hardee was still on the march from Averasboro, and some of the promised troops from the Army of Tennessee had not arrived, Johnston could wait no longer. In another day all three of the Union columns—each numbering more than 20,000 men—would meet at Goldsboro, while Johnston would have only a third as many soldiers even after Hardee arrived. Johnston's best chance was to defeat one of Sherman's columns before the others could come to its aid. The Federal right and left wings

were reported to be more than a day's march apart, with Schofield even farther away. Now was the time to strike, and Slocum's left wing would be the target.

Wade Hampton's cavalrymen were watching from a distance as Slocum's advance passed just south of Bentonville. There Hampton had found terrain that he thought would be ideal for a Confederate attack. The trick would be to delay the Federals until Johnston could occupy the ground.

All day on March 18, Hampton's riders skirmished with the enemy, forcing them to deploy and slowing them down. By late afternoon the Confederates had been pushed back to a position just in front of the wooded ridge Hampton had selected for the infantry, but the infantry had not yet arrived. Hampton unlimbered his horse artillery, dismounted his men, formed a line in the open and made an ostentatious show of preparing to fight Slocum's 20,000 Federals with his 3,000 troopers. "I knew that if a serious attack was made on me the guns would be lost," Hampton said later, "but I determined to run this risk in the hope of checking the Federal advance." As his men awaited the Federal reaction, a Confederate remarked to his comrades: "Old Hampton is playing a bluff game, and if he don't mind, Sherman will call him."

But after making what Hampton called a "feeble" demonstration, the lead Federals went into camp to wait for the rest of the left wing to arrive that night. Hampton was satisfied: "We were thus left in possession of the ground chosen for the fight."

Sherman, who had been riding with Slocum's wing, had decided to cut across to Howard's right wing, still several miles distant. Told that only cavalry was confronting Slocum, he rode away on the morning of March 19, confident that no serious encounter was imminent. Slocum ordered the division of Brigadier General William P. Carlin to sweep away the Confederate opposition.

When Carlin's men advanced, they came under unexpectedly heavy artillery fire and

Brigadier General Judson Kilpatrick (*center*) urges his cavalry forward in a sudden counterattack to reclaim the headquarters near Fayetteville he had lost to raiding Confederates a few hours earlier. Charging with the recklessness that had earned him Sherman's admiration, "Little Kil" overran the surprised Confederates and recaptured the camp.

Captain Theodore F. Northrup commanded Kilpatrick's scouts on wide-ranging forays to gather intelligence, to destroy railroads and bridges — and sometimes to enrich themselves. The Episcopal Bishop of North Carolina identified Northrup as the leader of a raiding party that robbed him of his watch, jewelry, clothes and horse.

stopped to entrench. This accomplished, Carlin sent a strong skirmish line against the enemy's dismounted cavalry on the forward slope of the ridge, where it had been the night before. As expected, Hampton's troopers retreated behind the ridge. But when the Federals approached the thickly wooded crest, a blaze of musketry drove them back in astonishment. They advanced a second time, with the same result.

A Federal staff officer who had been watching the action hurried over to Slocum. This was no mere cavalry skirmish, he reported. There was "infantry entrenched along our whole front, and enough of them to give us all the amusement we shall want for the rest of the day." Slocum was, in fact, momentarily outnumbered. His men were still coming in from their long march of the day before, and only about 10,000 of them had arrived. They were confronting Johnston's entire force, which had come up during the night. Hardee's troops, the last to arrive, had started to deploy just as the battle was beginning.

Behind the ridge, in the cover of the woods and unnoticed by the inattentive Federals, Johnston had arrayed his infantry in a curving line that extended well beyond the Federal left. He now had his army organized in three corps. Bragg's men were positioned athwart the road to Goldsboro at its intersection with the road north to Smithfield; Hardee was assigned to the center, echeloned forward to Bragg's right (his troops had rushed into position while Bragg's men were repulsing Carlin's skirmishers); and Lieutenant General Alexander P. Stewart with 4,000 men from the Army of Tennessee held the right, his line parallel to the Goldsboro road and facing south. Hampton, after falling back through Bragg's lines, led his cavalry to the extreme right, looking for a chance to fall on the Federal rear.

The prospects for a crushing Confederate counterattack were ideal. But then Johnston made a mistake. General Bragg, afraid he could not withstand another attack, asked for reinforcements. Johnston immediately — and, he later acknowledged, "most injudiciously" — sent him one of Hardee's divisions. It turned out that Bragg did not need help after all — but Johnston could not attack until the division returned to its position. Thus he was not ready to move until midafternoon. By then Slocum had twice as many men on the field — all of XIV Corps and a few units from XX Corps — and they had prepared breastworks.

Carlin's Federals were entrenched facing northeast, toward Hoke's division, still unaware that the Confederate line extended far beyond their left. Another XIV Corps division, under Brigadier General James D. Morgan, had dug in on Carlin's right. Brigadier General James S. Robinson, who had just appeared with a XX Corps brigade, formed a second line behind Carlin.

At 3 p.m., Johnston launched his belated attack, with Hardee smashing into Carlin's front and Stewart's Tennesseans swinging around the Federal left. Hardee led his men in person as they made their charge, and the Federals retreated.

Their flight was triggered by the sound of Stewart's Confederates in their rear. Although a much-diminished force — "It was a painful sight," said an observer among Bragg's troops, "to see how close their battle flags were together" — the remaining troops of the Army of Tennessee did their duty that day, falling on the left and rear of

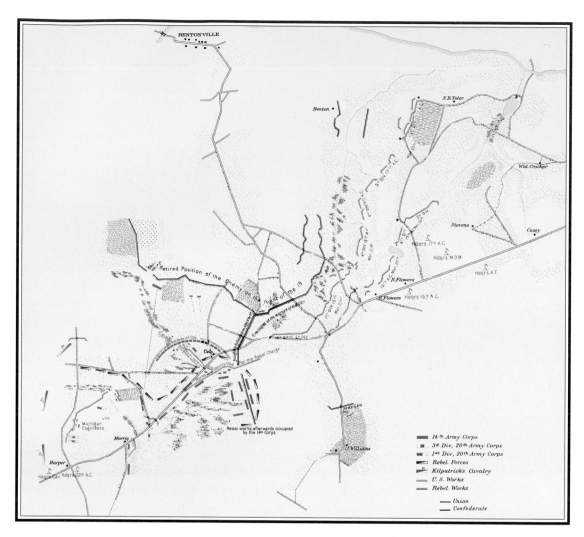

This contemporary U.S. Army map shows the positions held by Union and Confederate forces during the three days of battle at Bentonville, North Carolina. On March 19, Johnston's Confederates massed to destroy Slocum's two Federal corps, the left wing of Sherman's army. Slocum's advance division pressed Hampton's cavalry, only to be hit by a massive Confederate attack. The Federals entrenched and stopped several determined assaults, forcing Johnston to retire behind Mill Creek by evening. The next day brought little fighting, but Sherman's right wing moved into position late in the afternoon and attacked on the following morning. The Confederates held fast but, vastly outnumbered, they retreated from the field that night.

Carlin's division and Robinson's brigade. The unnerved Federals gave way in a retreat that, Lieutenant Charles Brown recalled sardonically, "was the best thing we done that whole day," and involved "some of the best running ever did." The XIV Corps emblem was an acorn, and other Federal units later took delight in dubbing the engagement the "Battle of Acorn Run."

But the rout was short-lived. On encountering some approaching XX Corps units, the Federals who had been in flight recovered their wits and, said one of them, "looked ashamed." Their retreat had exposed Morgan's division to attack from the rear, and Stewart's men now swept around behind them. At the same time, Bragg's corps advanced on Morgan's front.

Morgan's troops hunkered down and fought. They waited until Bragg's charge was within 30 yards of them, then opened a staggering fire that they maintained by forming two lines — one to shoot, one to load. They even managed a brief counterattack. Meanwhile, Brigadier General Jefferson C. Davis, commanding XIV Corps, sent Colonel Benjamin Fearing's brigade to hold off the Confederate sweep.

But Fearing did not have enough men to stem the tide. He retreated 300 yards before making a stand, and a gap opened in the Federal line. Hardee's Confederates sprinted into that break and joined in the attack on Morgan's rear. Davis, watching the action, told an aide, "If Morgan's troops can stand this, all is right. If not, all is lost. There is no reserve."

But reinforcements were closer than Davis realized. All the while, General Slocum had been urging XX Corps forward; one soldier

Brigadier General Laurence S. Baker led the 1st Brigade of the North Carolina Junior Reserves — soldiers not yet 18 years old — at Kinston and Bentonville. A West Point graduate and originally a cavalry officer, Baker had suffered wounds that rendered him unfit — first for cavalry service and later for any combat. He was summoned back to the field to take part in the desperate effort to stop Sherman.

Lieutenant General Alexander P. Stewart, appointed on March 16 to command the remnants of the Army of Tennessee, led his 4,000 men in Johnston's patchwork army at the Battle of Bentonville three days later. A modest professor of mathematics and philosophy in peacetime, Stewart was known to his troops as "Old Straight."

later marveled, "We actually ran eight miles without a halt." And now, just as the Confederates were about to overwhelm Morgan's hopelessly outnumbered men, a brigade under Colonel William Cogswell came in off the Goldsboro road.

Sent forward immediately to rescue Morgan, Cogswell's men advanced on the flank of Stewart's Tennesseans and pinched off the Confederate movement, driving most of Stewart's men back to the north. Other Confederates, however, continued the attack on Morgan, whose men were now forced to leap to the other side of their breastworks and continue firing. Their situation was complicated because many of the Confederates were wearing captured uniform coats, and the beleaguered Federals could barely distinguish between their reinforcements and the attackers, all of whom were coming from the same direction. Before long, however, they had weeded out the remaining enemy, again established their lines facing Bragg and been reinforced.

Carlin's reorganized division, bolstered by fresh XX Corps units, had stabilized the bent-back Federal left. But this line too had a flaw, a 400-yard gap between Robinson's three regiments on the right and Colonel William Hawley's brigade on the left. Into this gap Johnston launched attack after attack in an effort to retain the momentum. The Union artillery covering the gap was effective, however, and with every passing minute the Confederates' numerical advantage was being reduced. The swelling Federal ranks beat off five successive charges before evening.

Early in the day, as soon as Slocum had realized the danger he faced, he began sending messages of alarm to Sherman. Sherman had already started some of his units on their way toward Slocum. Now he ordered the rest of Howard's tired troops back on the road and dispatched a message to Slocum that rang with encouragement: "All of the right wing will move at moonrise toward Bentonville. Fortify and hold your position to the last, certain that all the army is coming to you as fast as possible."

The first troops of the right wing arrived at the town of Bentonville at dawn on the 20th of March; they had been much closer at hand than Johnston had thought. The remainder of Howard's men came up by late afternoon — some had marched 25 miles without stopping to rest. They moved down the Goldsboro road toward the Confederate rear, hoping to surprise the enemy. But Johnston had skirmishers out, and the sound of their firing alerted him to the new threat.

He quickly pulled his left flank back north of the road, thus protecting it from easy attack by the arriving Federals.

For the rest of the day the two armies remained in position, neither side willing to attack. Sherman, low on supplies and uncertain of Johnston's strength, was reluctant to fight an unnecessary battle; surely the Confederates must retire in any case.

But Johnston stayed on. He was in extreme peril — greatly outmanned, far from any secure base, his line of retreat threatened — and he knew it would be folly to attack the larger army, which was now well entrenched. But he felt that he still might aid the Confederate cause if he could lure Sherman into a costly assault. In the meantime, he gathered up his wounded and sent them to Smithfield for evacuation by rail. While Johnston held his position, Sherman fretted.

A flank attack by the 1st Division of the Federal XVII Corps overruns an artillery position on the Confederate left during the third day of fighting at Bentonville. However, the division was repulsed before long by a Confederate counterattack and then recalled by Sherman.

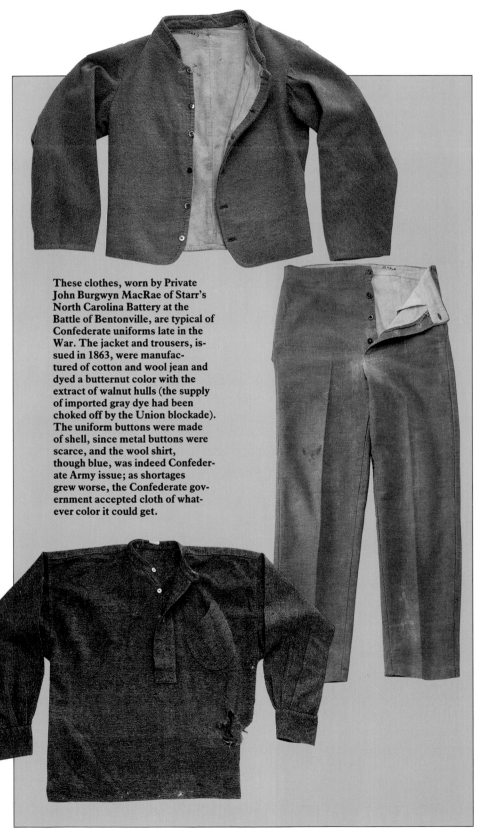

These clothes, worn by Private John Burgwyn MacRae of Starr's North Carolina Battery at the Battle of Bentonville, are typical of Confederate uniforms late in the War. The jacket and trousers, issued in 1863, were manufactured of cotton and wool jean and dyed a butternut color with the extract of walnut hulls (the supply of imported gray dye had been choked off by the Union blockade). The uniform buttons were made of shell, since metal buttons were scarce, and the wool shirt, though blue, was indeed Confederate Army issue; as shortages grew worse, the Confederate government accepted cloth of whatever color it could get.

"I cannot see why he remains," the Federal commander said in a note to Slocum.

The next day, March 21, began in much the same way. Although Johnston reported that "heavy skirmishing was renewed on the whole front," the two commanders stayed where they were, and for most of the day there was no full-scale attack by either side.

Then, unexpectedly, Sherman almost became embroiled in a general action in spite of himself. One of his favorite division commanders, the combative Major General Joseph A. Mower, slid around Johnston's left flank early in the afternoon on what was supposed to be a reconnaissance. But as Mower drove deeper, he found himself on the verge of cutting the potential Confederate line of retreat toward Smithfield. The Southern troops, reacting furiously, stopped Mower in a bloody fight. Among those who died in the encounter was General Hardee's 16-year-old son, whom Hardee had reluctantly allowed to join up only hours before the battle; among those who grieved the boy's death was Federal General Oliver Howard, who had taught Willie Hardee in Sunday school at West Point before the War.

Mower was preparing to continue the battle when Sherman, still unwilling to fight if it could be avoided, recalled him. It was a move Sherman subsequently regretted. "I think I made a mistake there," he admitted. If he had supported Mower instead of checking him, Sherman might have administered a smashing defeat to the Confederates.

As it was, Mower's attack may have been the last straw for Johnston. Most of his wounded were now safe, and Mower had demonstrated the magnitude of the danger. On March 22, the Federals awakened to find the Confederate army gone. On leaving,

Johnston had sent a harshly realistic message to Lee: "Sherman's course cannot be hindered by the small force I have. I can do no more than annoy him."

On the 23rd, Sherman's force joined Schofield's corps at Goldsboro. The railroad to New Bern was almost ready to be put back in operation, and Sherman's men no longer would have to live off the land. The soldiers, many of them ragged and barefoot, were issued new clothing. They also received their first mail in two months; 514 bags of it arrived over a two-day period.

Sherman needed to review his plans. An aide reported that Sherman "guessed he would go round to see Grant," who, said Sherman, had been "so long behind fortifications that he had got fossilized." Sherman "was going to stir him up." He left Goldsboro on March 25. To some soldiers who met him en route and clamorously asked what he was up to, he explained: "I'm going up to see Grant for five minutes and have it all chalked out for me and then come back and pitch in."

Late in the afternoon on the 27th, Sherman arrived by steamer at City Point. Grant and a few members of his staff were on hand to meet the red-haired Ohioan as he stepped ashore; the two chief officers of the Federal Army greeted each other, recalled Lieutenant Colonel Horace Porter, "like two schoolboys coming together after a vacation," grinning and shaking hands and making little jokes. "I didn't expect to find all you fellows here," Sherman said. "You don't travel as fast as we do."

The group repaired to Grant's headquarters, where Sherman paid his respects to Mrs. Grant. Then, sitting beside a campfire, Sherman entertained the assembled officers with the account of his Carolina adventures. After an hour Grant mentioned that Lincoln was also at City Point; perhaps, he said, they should call on him before dinner.

They found the President sitting alone in the after cabin of the *River Queen,* and once again Sherman had to tell his story of the Carolinas Campaign. This historic first, a joint meeting of the three principal actors on the Union side of the Civil War, was a "good, long social visit," Sherman said later.

The next day Grant, Sherman and Rear Admiral David D. Porter met with Lincoln to discuss the strategy they planned to use against Lee and Johnston. Lincoln repeatedly expressed the hope that no more blood need be shed, but both generals said they expected the Confederates to fight at least one more major battle.

Then a subject came up that was much on everyone's mind. The War was almost over; it was clear that not only the Confederate armies in the field but also the Confederate political authorities would be compelled to surrender soon. But no guidelines had been drawn. Unless some policy were spelled out in advance, the generals were likely to find themselves confronting a situation for which they were totally unprepared.

Sherman, by his own account, asked what the President meant to do with the defeated soldiers and the leaders of the Confederate government. "He said he was all ready," Sherman recalled. "All he wanted of us was to defeat the opposing armies, and to get the men composing the Confederate armies back to their homes, and work on their farms and in their shops." Admiral Porter quoted Lincoln as saying: "Let them once surrender and reach their homes, they won't take up arms again. Let them go, officers and all. I

General Sherman (*near left*) argues a point with General Grant, President Lincoln and Admiral David D. Porter during their meeting to discuss strategy and peace terms aboard the steamer *River Queen* in late March of 1865. Porter later wrote of Lincoln's attitude toward the South: "His heart was all tenderness."

want submission and no more bloodshed."

As for what was to become of Jefferson Davis, Lincoln hinted that he hoped Davis would leave the country, although he obviously could not say so in public. Lincoln illustrated his point with a story. It seems that a man who had taken a pledge of abstinence was offered a drink by a friend. He declined it, but agreed to accept a glass of lemonade. Then the friend suggested that the lemonade would taste better with a drop of brandy in it. The guest, said Lincoln, replied that if his host could add the brandy "unbeknown" to him he would not object. "I inferred," said Sherman, "that Mr. Lincoln wanted Davis to escape, 'unbeknown' to him."

Lincoln was clear about one point — and both Sherman and Porter remembered it distinctly. As soon as the fighting stopped, the people of the South "would at once be guaranteed all their rights" as citizens of a common country. "I want no one punished," Porter remembered him saying; "treat them liberally all around. We want those people to return to their allegiance to the Union and submit to the laws."

There was Sherman's answer. That afternoon, he boarded a swift boat for the return journey to Goldsboro. He was ready to wind up his end of the War, and he was certain now that he knew exactly on what terms Abraham Lincoln intended to finish it.

Waterloo of the Confederacy

"Before the last assault was made, the battle flags of the enemy made almost a solid line of bunting around the fort. The noise outside was fearful, frightful and indescribable, the curses and groaning of frenzied men could be heard over and above the din of our musketry. Savage men, ravenous beasts!"

CAPTAIN A. K. JONES, 16TH MISSISSIPPI IN THE DEFENSE OF FORT GREGG

After months of deadlock at Petersburg and belligerent maneuvering in the Carolinas, the shape of the spring campaign of 1865 emerged with breathtaking suddenness during four eventful days in March. On Thursday, March 23, the Federal armies of Sherman and John M. Schofield united at Goldsboro, North Carolina, and General Joseph Johnston confessed his inability to prevent their joining Grant in Virginia. On Friday, Grant drew up his plan for yet another flanking movement against the Confederate right below Petersburg. It was to be the first large-scale operation of the year, and it was to begin five days hence.

On Saturday, General Gordon's attack on Fort Stedman failed to ease the remorseless Federal pressure on the Army of Northern Virginia. And on Sunday, March 26, General Lee informed President Davis that Richmond and Petersburg were doomed; Lee felt he had to get the army away, join forces with Johnston and continue the fight elsewhere.

Somehow, Lee would have to move his 57,000 remaining men safely out of their trenches and off to the southwest without becoming ensnared in a general engagement with Grant's 125,000 troops. From Petersburg, Lee knew he had to follow the Southside Railroad — its battered rolling stock would be needed if he was to get everyone and everything away — to its junction with the Richmond & Danville Railroad at Burke Station. From there he could follow the Danville line to the southwest and to Johnston. If he waited too long, Grant's legions would swarm all over him.

On the Sunday that Lee announced it was time to go, the advantage in numbers already enjoyed by the Federals was increased; Major General Philip H. Sheridan rode in from the Shenandoah Valley with 5,700 cavalrymen. Sheridan had defeated the last remnant of Jubal Early's Army of the Valley at Waynesboro on March 2. He had gone on to destroy the railroads around Lynchburg and then had headed toward Richmond. "Feeling that the War was nearing its end," Sheridan wrote later in his memoirs, "I desired my cavalry to be in at the death."

Grant was delighted by Sheridan's combativeness and impressed by his willingness to give up his independent department (the vast Middle Military Division) and revert to his former assignment as commander of the Army of the Potomac's cavalry. The corps now consisted of three divisions: the two Sheridan had brought back from the Valley, now commanded by Brigadier Generals Thomas C. Devin and George A. Custer, both of whom reported to Brevet Major General Wesley Merritt, and the 3,300-man division that had stayed at Petersburg, now led by Major General George Crook. Grant would assign the cavalry a principal role — and the status of an independent army — in the impending campaign.

For more than a month, Grant had been

CHARLES CITY CROSS ROADS.

ANTIETAM. 1ST FREDERICKSBURG.

GETTYSBURG. RAPPAHANNOCK STATION.

61ST REG: P.V.

WILDERNESS. SPOTTSYLVANIA.

WASHINGTON JULY 12,1864 CHARLESTOW

CEDAR CREEK. PETERSBURG 2

Sergeant Joseph Fisher of the 61st Pennsylvania was awarded the Medal of Honor for carrying this regimental color in the vanguard of the attack that broke through the Confederate lines at Petersburg on April 2, 1865. A bursting shell shattered one of Fisher's arms and ripped open his side, but he crawled forward with the flag until he collapsed from loss of blood.

expecting Lee to attempt a juncture with Johnston, and he had planned a massive movement to prevent it. As a preliminary, General Ord was to pull one of his two corps — the XXIV, led by Major General John Gibbon — and Brigadier General Ranald Mackenzie's cavalry division out of the Federal lines north of the James River. They were to march south behind the position held by IX Corps and then west behind VI Corps to the Federal left, southwest of Petersburg. There, Ord's 15,000 men were to spread themselves thin and relieve from duty in the trenches both II Corps and V Corps, thus freeing the 35,000 men of those corps for Grant's proposed maneuver.

The field of operations envisioned by Grant was a rectangle southwest of Petersburg that was 10 miles across, east to west, and eight miles deep. It was bounded on the north by the Southside Railroad; on the east by the Weldon Railroad; on the south by the Vaughan road to the village of Dinwiddie Court House; and on the west by a road leading north from Dinwiddie to the Southside Railroad — by way of a crossroads called Five Forks. The sector was cut diagonally by the Boydton Plank Road between Petersburg and Dinwiddie and by Hatcher's Run, flowing northwest to southeast.

Confederate entrenchments extended into this area from Petersburg, running south-

west along the Boydton Plank Road to its crossing of Hatcher's Run — the center of the rectangle. From there the White Oak road led west to Five Forks; the fortifications followed it for two miles, then curved north to touch Hatcher's Run again. The Federal left, despite frequent attempts to extend it westward, was still located on the Vaughan road where it crossed Hatcher's Run, four miles southeast of the Confederate right.

When relieved by Ord's men, General Warren's V Corps, followed by General Humphreys' II Corps, was to march five miles west along the Vaughan road until the troops were beyond the Confederate flank. From there the infantry was to press north toward the enemy line. They were not to attack it, however; the object was to flank the Confederates, forcing them to come out of their trenches to protect their rear and the Southside Railroad. Most important, Grant emphasized, the infantry was to ensure the success of Sheridan's cavalry.

The plan called for the cavalry to swing below and beyond the moving infantry, to Dinwiddie Court House, then north toward Five Forks, working behind the Confederate line. What happened next would depend on Lee. In the unlikely event that he did not come out of his lines and fight, Sheridan was to destroy both the Southside and Danville Railroads around Burkeville, cutting Lee's last supply line and escape route.

On the morning of March 29, when General Lee learned that the Federal movements were under way, he was instantly aware of what they portended and he reacted as strongly as he could. He had already pulled an infantry division under Major General George E. Pickett from Longstreet's corps

south of the James to assist in the attack on Fort Stedman. Pickett had not arrived in time to be of help, but now his 5,000 men were available to bolster General Richard Anderson on the Confederate right. (After Longstreet had recovered from the near-fatal wound he suffered at the Wilderness and resumed command of I Corps the previous fall, Anderson had been given the makeshift, division-size IV Corps.)

But to counter Sheridan, Lee needed more horsemen. He summoned his nephew, Major General Fitzhugh Lee, whose cavalry had been guarding the Confederate left, to join and take overall charge of the divisions led by Major General William H. F. (Rooney) Lee, the commanding general's son, and Brigadier General Thomas Rosser. Their combined force of about 5,500 troopers would have to take on Sheridan's 11,000. Lee then had Anderson send out Major General Bushrod Johnson's division to determine the identity and strength of the Federal

infantry that was advancing from the south on the Quaker road.

It was Warren's V Corps, with the division of Brigadier General Charles Griffin in the lead, groping north from the Vaughan road. The Federals were moving through nasty country — flat, clayey, poorly drained ground obstructed by dense brush. Rain had raised the marshy streams that veined the area and had softened the convoluted trails. And on March 29 it was raining again. "We went slipping and plunging through the black slimy mud in which pointed rocks were bedded," a Federal marcher recalled, "now stumbling over a rotten tree, now over the stiffening corpse of some poor comrade by whose side we might soon lie."

At midafternoon, Griffin's lead brigade — that of Brigadier General Joshua Lawrence Chamberlain — was approaching a sawmill on the Quaker road, just north of Gravelly Run, when it encountered Bushrod Johnson's Confederates. The slender 36-year-old

Accompanied by his top commanders, Major General Philip H. Sheridan questions a black man at Dinwiddie Court House on March 29, 1865. Earlier in the day, Sheridan's cavalry had seized the town, five miles southeast of Five Forks, as part of a flanking movement designed to force Lee's army out of its entrenchments at Petersburg.

Chamberlain had seen more than his share of fighting since leaving the faculty of Bowdoin College to become a field officer in the 20th Maine. He had been wounded at Petersburg nine months earlier and still was not fully recovered. During the fierce engagement that now developed, Chamberlain was hit again. His horse was rearing at the time, and the bullet passed first through the animal's neck, then ripped Chamberlain's left sleeve and slammed into his chest, where it was deflected by a leather case and a mirror Chamberlain carried in his breast pocket. The shot coursed along his ribs, passed out the back seam of his coat, and went on to unhorse a staff officer riding behind him. Knocked unconscious, Chamberlain recovered seconds later to find General Griffin supporting him. "My dear General," said Griffin, "you are gone." Chamberlain raised his head, saw his men retreating and said, "Yes, General, I am."

But a moment later Chamberlain struggled onto his bleeding horse and returned to the battle. Hatless and blood-smeared — the wounds of horse and rider had resulted, Chamberlain observed, in "a blood relationship of which I was not ashamed" — he rallied his brigade and regained the lost ground.

That evening, with the rain slashing down, Grant either sensed an opportunity, or came to a long-deferred decision: He abruptly changed Sheridan's orders. Forget the railroads, Grant said; instead, stay close to the infantry. "In the morning push around the enemy, if you can, and get on his right rear. We will act together as one army until it is seen what can be done." Grant still offered no definite plan of action, but he was clear on one point, which he made in a casual, artless sentence: "I feel now like ending the matter, if it is possible to do so, before going back."

The goal was simply stated, but not easily accomplished. The heavy rain continued on the 30th, and movement was difficult. Nevertheless, Humphreys and Warren edged closer to the Confederate trenches, pressing the enemy but not assaulting. And Sheridan sent Merritt with Devin's cavalry division slogging northward from Dinwiddie to occupy the important intersection of Five Forks, directly on Lee's probable escape route.

About halfway there, the Federals ran into Fitzhugh Lee's troopers — who had arrived at Five Forks that morning — and became engaged in heavy skirmishing. The rain was turning the countryside into a morass. "The troops waded in mud above their ankles," said Lieutenant Colonel Horace Porter, Grant's aide-de-camp. "Horses sank to their bellies, and wagons threatened to disappear altogether." Grant, at his headquarters behind II Corps near Gravelly Run, watched in frustration. To move artillery forward, the roads would have to be corduroyed. The men started calling to their officers in grim jest: "Fetch along the pontoons" and "When are the gunboats coming up?"

At noon on the 30th, Grant sent word that Sheridan should call off the next day's operations. "The heavy rain of today will make it impossible for us to do much until it dries up a little." Sheridan was dismayed. He was ready to fight, and he wanted no delays. That afternoon he rode through the downpour to Grant's headquarters, seven miles away, his horse "plunging at every step almost to the knees in the mud." There he regaled a group of staff officers with an excited defense of the original plan, pacing up and down, said Porter, like a hound on a leash.

"I can drive in the whole cavalry force of the enemy with ease," Sheridan exclaimed. Furthermore, he said, if he were given infantry he could roll up the Confederate flank or exert enough pressure to make possible a breakthrough elsewhere. "I tell you," Sheridan said fiercely, "I'm ready to strike out tomorrow and go to smashing things!"

Sheridan's enthusiasm was catching, and his listeners urged him to talk to Grant. The two generals met in Grant's tent, and after Sheridan had made his case, Grant gave in. "We will go on," he said. Elated, Sheridan hurried away to get the operation moving.

Upon returning to his own camp at Dinwiddie Court House late that afternoon, Sheridan ordered Merritt to develop the enemy's position and strength. Merritt dispatched a brigade northward and succeeded in driving the opposing cavalry back to Five Forks. But there the Federal horsemen found Confederate infantry — Pickett's division — entrenched and in a fighting mood. After a short exchange of fire, the Federals fell back and reported that the enemy intended to hold Five Forks.

In the evening, Sheridan notified Grant of the presence of Pickett's division. The two had discussed Sheridan's need for infantry support during their meeting that day. Sheridan had asked for Major General Horatio Wright's VI Corps, which had fought under him in the Shenandoah Valley. But VI Corps was miles away in the Petersburg trenches, beyond both V Corps and II Corps. Shifting three corps around in the rain and at night would be impossible, Grant told Sheridan. He could have Humphreys and II Corps, if he insisted, but V Corps was the obvious choice.

The problem was V Corps's commander,

Major General Gouverneur Kemble Warren. Warren had performed heroically at Gettysburg and was one of the most highly esteemed officers in the Army of the Potomac, yet he was beset by flaws that hampered his ability to work smoothly with his fellow officers. High-strung and temperamental at best, Warren had become increasingly abrasive as the War went on, his moods alternating between rage and sulking lethargy. "I am becoming more than ever convinced that he has a screw loose," wrote V Corps artillery chief Charles Wainwright, "and is not quite accountable for all his freaks." Sheridan did not want Warren, and Grant could see why. The matter remained unresolved overnight, and the next morning Sheridan was far too busy to pursue it.

The Confederacy might be almost on its knees, but Robert E. Lee had not changed. Facing overwhelming odds and a critical threat to his position and communications, he decided to take the offensive.

The previous evening Lee had sent Pickett, with three of his own brigades and two of Anderson's, to join Fitzhugh Lee at Five Forks and drive Sheridan away. This was a heavy responsibility for Pickett, the dashing 40-year-old general whose greatest fame thus far in the War had come for leading a hopeless charge at Gettysburg; but Lee's choices were limited, and his need was great. While Pickett fought Sheridan, Lee would direct an attack on the Union infantry, with some of A. P. Hill's and Anderson's brigades striking V Corps on its left flank.

The rain stopped at last on the morning of the 31st, and Merritt sent Devin's cavalry north to locate the enemy so Sheridan could "go to smashing things." Crook's men were

By 1 p.m. on the 1st of April, Sheridan had deployed Federal cavalry under Wesley Merritt in front of George Pickett's Confederates, who were entrenched at Five Forks. Sheridan planned to pin down Pickett with the cavalry while Warren's V Corps assaulted the Angle on the Confederate left. It was 4 p.m. before Warren came into action, and because of faulty deployment, V Corps nearly missed its objective. Despite the confusion and delay, Warren's attack struck Pickett a decisive blow; by 7 p.m. the Confederate force had been virtually destroyed.

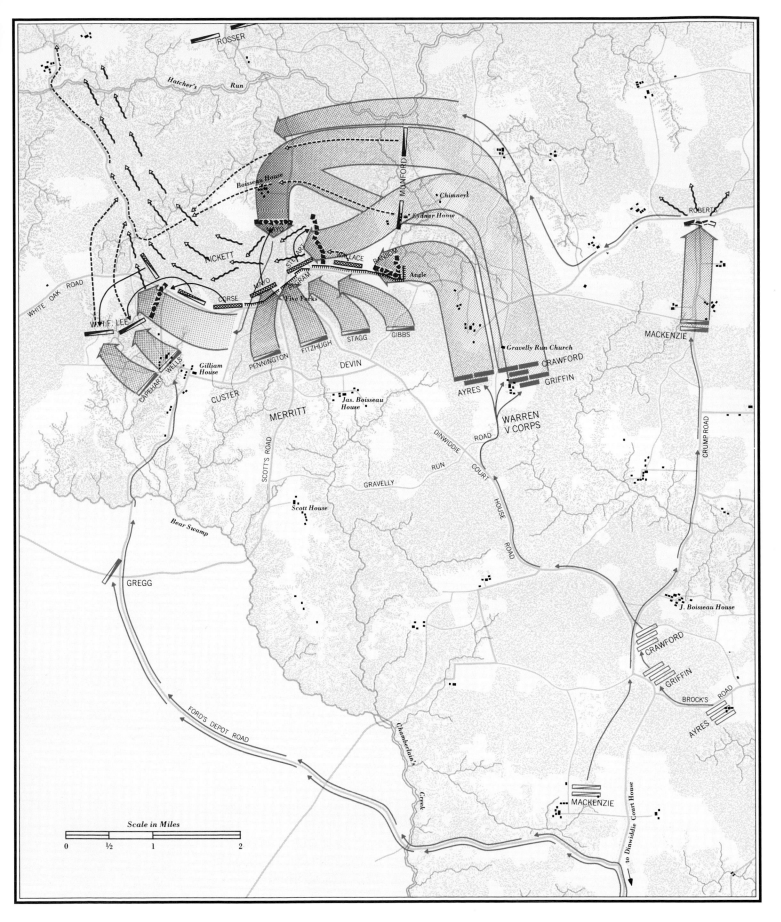

ROSSER

Hatcher's   Run

Boisseau House

MUNFORD

Chimneys

Sydnor House

PICKETT   STUART   WALLACE   RANSOM

CORSE   MAYO   PEGRAM   Angle

WM.F.LEE   Five Forks

CAPEHART   WELLS   PENNINGTON   FITZHUGH   STAGG   GIBBS

WHITE   OAK   ROAD   Gilliam   House   DEVIN

Gravelly Run Church

CRAWFORD

AYRES   GRIFFIN

CUSTER

MERRITT   Jas. Boisseau
House   WARREN
V CORPS

ROBERTS

MACKENZIE

SCOTT'S   ROAD   DINWIDDIE   COURT   HOUSE   ROAD   CRUMP   ROAD

GRAVELLY   RUN

Scott House

Bear Swamp

J. Boisseau House

GREGG

CRAWFORD

GRIFFIN

BROCK'S   ROAD

AYRES

FORD'S DEPOT ROAD

Chamberlain's

Creek

MACKENZIE

to Dinwiddie Court House

Scale in Miles

0   ½   1   2

in position to defend Dinwiddie, and Custer's were escorting the bogged-down Federal wagon train six miles to the east.

By noon, Sheridan's confidence had become consternation; besides the enemy cavalry on the road to Five Forks, his patrols had discovered a large force of Pickett's infantry heading toward Dinwiddie, around his left. Instead of attacking at his leisure, Sheridan was going to have to defend himself. Hastily, he sent two of Crook's mounted brigades to meet the threat from the west.

About 2 p.m. the Confederate flanking force hit hard, driving one of Crook's bri-

gades and two of Devin's nearly a mile east, all the way across the Dinwiddie road. There Pickett wheeled his men and advanced south toward the village, while Rosser's and Rooney Lee's cavalry divisions assailed the Federals from the west. Pickett's plan of attack had been well conceived, and he was executing it flawlessly. As the afternoon wore on, two of Sheridan's brigades, led by Alfred Gibbs and J. Irvin Gregg, fought stubbornly to hold their advanced position on the Dinwiddie road, but the Confederate infantry drove them steadily south.

Sheridan coolly arranged for the reconcen-

Two brigades of George Armstrong Custer's 3rd Cavalry Division charge a line of Virginians on the Confederate far right at Five Forks. "Before the enemy could shift his batteries, my columns were moving rapidly to place themselves in the rear of his position," Custer reported. "The retreat of over 5,000 of the rebels was then cut off."

tration of his scattered units and called up Custer from his escort duties with two fresh brigades. Forming a defensive line on the last rise of ground north of the village, Custer withstood two assaults, then counterattacked before darkness ended the fighting. It would surely resume in the morning, and Sheridan was in a perilous position.

Meanwhile, General Warren, to the east, had been having his own troubles — and the enemy was only part of them. The previous day, after having been confounded by contradictory marching orders, Warren had suggested that he put a force across the White Oak road, thus isolating Pickett's troops from the Confederate right.

Warren's proposal had been approved by Meade, and on the morning of the 31st, before Sheridan realized how much trouble he was in, Warren sent out a division under Major General Romeyn B. Ayres to see how strongly the White Oak road was defended. The men marched into the jaws of Anderson's flanking attack.

Anderson's force was a hodgepodge — four brigades drawn from three divisions — with tactical command falling to Bushrod Johnson. They were not quite in place when Ayres's Federals began to cross the road. In the vanguard was a brigade of New York Zouaves and Heavy Artillerymen, led by Brevet Brigadier General Frederic Winthrop. They were met by a volley of musketry from Colonel Martin Stansel's Alabama brigade, then were charged on the left flank by Brigadier General Eppa Hunton's Virginians. Winthrop's men gave way, and the other brigades of Ayres's division collapsed in succession before the ferocious onslaught. When Samuel Crawford's division came to Ayres's relief, it was routed in turn.

The third of Warren's divisions, commanded by General Griffin, had started the day in reserve; its soldiers were basking in the welcome sunshine when the sound of battle broke their reverie. Griffin got his men moving toward the fighting, only to be confronted by a mass of fugitives from the two other divisions. "For God's sake," Griffin shouted, "let them through or they will break our line!" But Griffin's line held and, bolstered by artillery, halted the Confederate advance. Meanwhile, on V Corps's right, Brigadier General Nelson A. Miles led his division of II Corps in an advance that regained some of the lost ground.

By midafternoon Warren was ready to mount a counterattack, assigning the task to Joshua Chamberlain's brigade. "Will you save the honor of the V Corps?" Warren asked in a voice tight with emotion. So Chamberlain, still in pain from his wound, led a furious charge that not only restored the line but surged ahead to the White Oak road. The attack evoked the admiration of both friend and foe; "I thought," said Confederate General Eppa Hunton, "it was one of the most gallant things I have ever seen."

It was now late in the day. The Federal infantry had made little progress, and the cavalry was in trouble. Warren heard the firing from Dinwiddie Court House and, without waiting for orders, sent a brigade to help Sheridan fend off Pickett. Sheridan needed the help: "This force is too strong for us," he admitted in a message to Grant. Yet the situation held an incomparable opportunity for the Federals. Sheridan saw it, even as his troopers fell back toward Dinwiddie, and explained it to Colonel Porter, who had ridden over to assess the situation for Grant.

Pickett's force, Sheridan insisted, "is in

more danger than I am — if I am cut off from the Army of the Potomac, it is cut off from Lee's army, and not a man in it should ever be allowed to go back to Lee. We at last have drawn the enemy's infantry out of its fortifications, and this is our chance to attack it." But Sheridan needed infantry, and again he pleaded for VI Corps, refusing to accept the impossibility of such a movement.

A deluge of orders had been raining down on Warren. First he was told to withdraw from the day's advances and to send a brigade to Sheridan — which, of course, he had already done. But circumstances were thwarting any attempt at efficient movement. The streams were running high and the bridge over Gravelly Run, on the Boydton Plank Road to Dinwiddie, was out. Orders, suggesting other routes and then demanding a full division for Sheridan, were coming at Warren from a variety of sources — Meade, Grant and Sheridan — and they were, in Chamberlain's words, "to an amazing degree confused and conflicting." Warren's men were bone-tired, and the weather had turned stormy again. The simple process of sending instructions was a problem: Maps were poor, the terrain was thickly wooded and the enemy was close by.

Yet in all this confusion, General Warren also realized that Pickett was vulnerable. At 8:40 p.m., Warren suggested that he move his entire corps west and attack the Confederates on one side while Sheridan assailed the other. An hour later, Meade relayed the idea to Grant. Warren could send Griffin's division down the Boydton Plank Road, straight to Sheridan's support, and take his other two around to the enemy's rear by way of a parallel road a mile to the north. Grant approved: "Let Warren move in the way you propose,

and urge him not to stop for anything." Grant then told Sheridan that V Corps would be in position by midnight.

By the time Grant's approval was relayed back through Meade to Warren, it was almost 11 p.m. The bridge on the Boydton Plank Road was not repaired until 2 the next morning, and confusion between Meade and Warren over routes and priorities persisted even longer. It was nearly 6 a.m. before Warren finally got his remaining two divisions on the road.

At daybreak Pickett, seeing how exposed his position was, had begun to retreat, followed closely by Merritt's Federal cavalry. Sheridan sent urgent orders to Warren: He must attack at once. But the two divisions of V Corps that were to take the northern route

Major Generals George E. Pickett (*above*) and Fitzhugh Lee (*top*), the senior Confederate officers at Five Forks, were away from their posts, enjoying a shadbake at the headquarters of Brigadier General Thomas L. Rosser (*left*) near Hatcher's Run, when the Federals attacked. Their party ended abruptly when Union infantry appeared across the stream.

were just getting under way. They were in position by 7 a.m., but it was too late. Pickett was gone, and Sheridan was furious.

Merritt and the cavalry, having followed Pickett north, found him in his former entrenchments paralleling the White Oak road, centered on Five Forks. Sheridan devised a daring plan of attack. While the cavalry, fighting dismounted, feinted toward Pickett's right and pinned down his center, Warren's infantry would assault the left. If the Federals could turn that flank and drive the Confederates westward, they would be cut off from the rest of Lee's army.

Sheridan worked out a complicated movement for V Corps. Pickett had anticipated just such a flanking attack and had refused his left — bent it back at a 90-degree angle, or return, north of the White Oak road. Sheridan wanted V Corps to attack from the southeast, at a 45-degree angle to the main enemy line. General Crawford's division, on the right, would strike the angle of the Confederate breastworks while General Ayres's division, on the left, would slant in against the main line. Griffin's division would follow Crawford's to help force the angle.

When Warren finally found Sheridan at 1 p.m., the two generals discussed the new plan, as General Warren put it later, "until I understood it, I think; and he was convinced that I understood him." It was a meeting that would have unfortunate consequences.

Warren's demeanor bothered Sheridan. Time was passing; the corps was moving to its new position at Gravelly Run Church too slowly, Sheridan thought, and apparently nothing was being done to hurry the men. Sheridan's disappointment in Warren, he related, "grew into disgust." And when he told Warren he was afraid they would run out of daylight before the infantry attacked, he thought Warren responded with "apathy" and "indifference."

By the time Warren's exhausted soldiers finally began to arrive at their destination on Pickett's flank, Sheridan was all but consumed with impatience. "He made every possible appeal for promptness," Horace Porter said, "dismounted from his horse, paced up and down, and struck the clenched fist of one hand against the palm of the other, and fretted like a caged tiger."

The Confederates also were in some disarray. Despite the exposed nature of Pickett's position at Dinwiddie, Lee thought that he should have remained there, holding Sheridan well away from the vital Southside Railroad. Lee's orders to Pickett were unusually curt: "Regret exceedingly your forced withdrawal, and your inability to hold the advantage you had gained. Hold Five Forks at all hazards."

So Pickett, who had hoped to withdraw to a stronger defensive position behind Hatcher's Run, had returned to his old breastworks at Five Forks. Still, there had been no indication of Federal infantry throughout the day, and if the Federal cavalry attacked alone, the Confederates were sure they could fight the troopers off.

Blithely confident, Pickett and Fitzhugh Lee decided to indulge in a few hours of relaxation. It was spring, and the shad were running in the Nottoway River nearby; General Rosser had netted some of the delectable fish and had invited his two commanding officers to a shadbake at his headquarters on the north bank of Hatcher's Run. Pickett and Lee, as hungry as anyone in their army, eagerly accepted. Just before Lee left, he was accosted by Brigadier General Thomas Munford, one of his division commanders. Munford had received a dispatch that indicated Federal cavalry had severed their communications with Anderson's corps to the east. Lee dismissed the news and rode off with Pickett shortly after 2 p.m. The two officers told no one where they were going and appointed no one to command in their absence.

Rosser's feast was a leisurely one. Alcohol may have been served. Time passed. At 4:15 p.m., the Federal V Corps at last finished forming its lines of battle, in clear sight of the Confederate left. Munford immediately sent a courier to report the impending attack to Fitzhugh Lee or to Pickett. The rider could find neither of them. Subsequent messengers frantically combed the area for the missing commanders without success.

When the Federal assault came shortly afterward, the sound of battle did not carry the mile and a half to the site of the shadbake — perhaps owing to some "peculiar phenomenon of acoustic shadows," as Confederate artillery commander E. Porter Alexander later suggested. Thus the Confederates in Pickett's line had to face the onslaught with no one in overall command.

As it happened, the meticulously planned Federal attack misfired. The Confederate angle, concealed in thick woods, was a full 800 yards farther west than Sheridan had thought, and the oblique Federal advance almost missed it. The vital spot was struck not by the massed weight of Crawford's and Griffin's divisions on the Federal right but by Ayres's smaller force, on the left.

Ayres had to wheel sharply to the left, under fire, to face the enemy's refused flank. Crawford and Griffin marched past the angle. Off to their right, Munford's Confederate cavalry was shooting, and Crawford's division headed toward this gunfire; Crawford missed the Confederate line entirely and marched away from the battle, with Griffin following close behind.

Joshua Chamberlain realized with mounting concern that his brigade was losing touch with Ayres. He was appalled to see Crawford in combat about 600 yards to the right while Ayres was fighting furiously about 600 yards to the left. "The great gap between these engagements," Chamberlain said, "made me feel that something was all wrong." He wheeled his brigade to the left and hurried toward the embattled Ayres. Griffin, quickly comprehending, followed Chamberlain with his other two brigades.

"The moment we showed our heads," Chamberlain wrote later, "we were at close quarters with the enemy." Indeed, Ayres and Griffin were virtually on top of the 150-yard-long line of breastworks held by Brigadier General Matthew Ransom's North Carolina brigade. Ironically, though, the Federals' error in direction and their remedial action had caused them to overlap the Confederate left flank and rear. Crawford was now marching westward through the woods, far behind the Confederate line.

Chamberlain encountered Sheridan near the angle, yelling reassurance to the lead elements of Ayres's division. "We'll get the twist on 'em, boys!" Sheridan cried. "There won't be a grease spot of 'em left!" But when the first Confederate fire struck the Federal ranks, the attack wavered. Suddenly Sheridan, a small figure on a large mount, was in front of them all. "He put spurs to his horse," wrote Horace Porter, "and dashed along in front of the line of battle." Yelling and waving, Sheridan galvanized the Federals with a relentless personal force. As they resumed their advance, a soldier near Sheridan fell to the ground, blood spurting from his neck. The man cried "I'm killed!" but Sheridan would not hear of it.

"You're not hurt a bit!" he declared. "Pick up your gun, man, and move right on to the front!"

The soldier clutched his weapon, said Porter, "and rushed forward a dozen paces before he fell, never to rise again."

As Ayres's men pushed forward, struggling through thick brush, another volley smashed into them. "They were staggered,"

said Porter, and "fell back in some confusion." Again Sheridan leaped to the fore. He seized his red-and-white personal flag and led the attackers, holding the banner high. "Bullets were now humming like a swarm of bees about our heads," wrote Porter, "and shells were crashing through the ranks. A musket-ball pierced the battle flag; another killed the sergeant who had carried it; another wounded an aide, Captain Andrew McGonnigle, in the side.

"All this time Sheridan was dashing from one point of the line to another, waving his

Confederate prisoners captured at Five Forks wait to be marched to the rear. "Droves of silent Johnnies, under guard, tramped through the mire," a Federal officer recalled, "jostling against noisy Yanks, who were filling the air with yells and catcalls — the effervescence of victory."

flag, shaking his fist, encouraging, entreating, threatening, praying, swearing, the very incarnation of battle.''

In the meantime, General Warren, having seen to it that Griffin was attacking along with Ayres, had gone after Crawford's division. He found it in the enemy rear, wheeled it and attacked southward. Beset from three sides, the Confederate line began to crumble. Captain Henry Chambers of the 49th North Carolina, in Ransom's brigade, was caught in the vortex of fire at the angle. "The minié balls were coming from both front and rear seemingly as thick as hail," Chambers recalled. "The poor wounded fellows were begging piteously to be carried off, and all this time the Yankee column in the rear was bearing down upon us." Ayres's and Griffin's men poured over the angle, officers and color-bearers in the lead. General Winthrop went down at the head of his New York brigade with a fatal wound in the lungs; Sheridan himself leaped his horse into the midst of a group of startled Confederates, who quickly surrendered.

General Pickett, still unaware of the battle raging nearby, was enjoying the afterglow of his feast. At length he decided to send a message to Five Forks. No sooner had his two couriers crossed Hatcher's Run than there was a burst of gunfire and the startled general saw one of the messengers being captured by Federal soldiers. Pickett, thoroughly alarmed, sprang to his horse and started at a gallop for Five Forks. He soon discovered that he was cut off from his command by the blueclad soldiers of Crawford's division. He appealed to Captain James Breckinridge of the 3rd Virginia Cavalry, who led a charge against the Federals to open a path for the returning general; the captain was killed, but Pickett got through.

When he reached the field, Pickett found that his left had been crushed and his force was being driven west; Crawford had cut the Ford's Depot road, Pickett's line of retreat to the north. Desperately, Pickett pulled Colonel Joseph Mayo's brigade out of line, faced it north and tried to hold off Crawford, but the Confederates almost immediately lost four guns and were driven back.

Merritt's Federal cavalry had been pressing Pickett from the south, the troopers fighting dismounted and blazing away with their carbines at any exposed opponent. Colonel William Johnson Pegram, the brilliant 23-year-old whom many considered the finest artillerist in the Army of Northern Virginia, had just told his gunners to "fire your canister low," when he pitched from his horse with a mortal wound. He died the next morning, less than two months after his older brother, General John Pegram, had fallen at Hatcher's Run.

While much of his force disintegrated in panic around him, Pickett made a final stand with Brigadier General Montgomery Corse's Virginia brigade. This rear guard opened a savage fire on Crawford's troops, who had wheeled to the west in pursuit. When General Warren saw his lines waver, he seized the flag of V Corps and spurred his gray horse to the forefront of the charge. Warren's horse was shot from under him, and Warren himself would have been killed or wounded had not Lieutenant Colonel Hollon Richardson of the 7th Wisconsin thrown himself in front of his commander, taking the bullet meant for Warren. Cheering wildly, Crawford's brigades rolled over Corse's Virginians.

By 6:45 p.m., the last Confederate resis-

tance had collapsed. Merritt's dismounted troopers advanced from the south, Custer led two brigades in a mounted charge from the west and Ranald Mackenzie's cavalry swept in from the east, routing what remained of Fitzhugh Lee's horsemen. More than 5,000 Confederates had been captured, along with 13 flags and six guns. "It has been an evil day for us," Captain Chambers wrote in his diary; "My heart sickens as I contemplate recording this day's disasters." General Munford would later call Five Forks "the Waterloo of the Confederacy."

At 7 p.m, as the gunfire diminished and darkness descended, Sheridan climaxed the day's drama by removing General Warren from command of V Corps. Throughout the day, Sheridan had expressed open dissatisfaction with Warren, fretting over his tardiness, criticizing his dispositions, questioning his aggressiveness. After he committed Crawford's division, Warren had sent a staff officer to Sheridan with an exuberant message: He was in the Confederates' rear, had cut off their retreat and was capturing many men. Sheridan's rejoinder had stunned Warren's aide.

"By God, sir," Sheridan snapped. "Tell General Warren he wasn't in that fight!" Soon afterward, encountering General Griffin, Sheridan told him to take command of V Corps. When the word reached Warren a short time later, he went to Sheridan — "with almost the agony of death upon his face," said Chamberlain — and asked him to reconsider. "Reconsider, hell!" said Sheridan. "I don't reconsider my decisions. Obey the order!"

And so Warren, his Army career demolished in the waning days of the War, reported to Grant for reassignment. He wound up commanding garrison troops and campaigning for a court of inquiry.

Word of the victory at Five Forks was conveyed to General Grant by Colonel Porter. As Porter rode away from the battlefield, he found the roads jammed with wagons, ambulances and celebrating soldiers. "Cheers were resounding on all sides," he said, "and everybody was riotous over the victory." Porter picked his way through the throngs and galloped into Grant's camp. "I began shouting the good news," Porter wrote, "and in a moment all but the imperturbable general-in-chief were on their feet, giving vent to boisterous demonstrations of joy. Dignity was thrown to the winds." These officers had seen many victories, but this one presaged the War's end.

Colonel Porter leaped from his horse and

found himself "rushing up to the general-in-chief and clapping him on the back with my hand, to his no little astonishment, and to the evident amusement of those about him." Grant endured Porter's enthusiasm without comment and read Sheridan's dispatch. He then turned to General Meade and said quietly, "Very well, then, I want Wright and Parke to assault tomorrow morning at four."

The Federal troops in the entrenchments outside Petersburg had been anticipating the order to attack for several days. General Lewis Grant, the hard-fighting commander of VI Corps's Vermont Brigade, had noted a diminishing number of Confederate soldiers in the works to his front and had urged General Wright to risk a limited offensive. Wright met with Meade, who personally reconnoitered the enemy lines and decided that an even larger assault was feasible. On the night of April 1, the generals readied their men for a supreme effort.

The soldiers received their orders with fatalistic determination, recalling all too well the futile sacrifices of earlier assaults. As the 14,000 men of VI Corps formed up in the chill darkness southwest of Petersburg, Major Hazard Stevens heard one soldier say to his comrades, "Well, good-by boys; this means death." Captain Thomas Beals of IX Corps, which would advance from the southeast against the most formidable portion of the defenses, later wrote, "There can be no doubt that few of us expected to emerge alive from this affair: for one, I did not."

Once Meade's forces were formed for the attack, the Union artillery opened with the greatest bombardment of the 10-month siege. "From hundreds of cannons, field guns and mortars came a stream of living fire," recalled Sergeant Joseph Gould of the 48th Pennsylvania; "the shells screamed through the air in a semi-circle of flame." The noisy barrage drowned out the sound of the signal gun at Fort Fisher that was to start the assault. It was nearly 5 a.m. before some units got under way.

The attack was spearheaded by teams of ax-wielding pioneers, the so-called forlorn hope, who were to chop a way through the bristling hedge of abatis and chevaux-de-frise that screened the enemy earthworks. Behind the pioneers, the massive columns of infantry marched forward with fixed bayonets. Muskets were loaded, but uncapped — to prevent unnecessary firing; haversacks and canteens had been left behind to avoid the telltale clanking that might alert the Confederates to the enemy's approach. "Nothing could be heard," Major Stevens noted, "save the sound of a deep, distant rustling, like a strong breeze blowing through the swaying boughs and dense foliage of some great forest." Startled Confederate pickets opened a scattering fire on the shadowy figures in front of them, then ran back to their lines, shouting the alarm. Soon the Federal ranks were raked with lead, but the attackers surged forward with cheers and a growing sense that perhaps this time their efforts would prevail. Lieutenant Colonel Robert Orr of the 61st Pennsylvania expressed the mood of every Union soldier when he wrote, "It was a great relief, a positive lifting of a load of misery to be at last let at them."

Parke's IX Corps was first to reach the Confederate works, battling John Gordon's corps for possession of Fort Mahone, a strong point known to the Federals as "Fort Damnation." The place lived up to its reputation: Hundreds of charging Federals went down beneath volleys of musketry and salvos

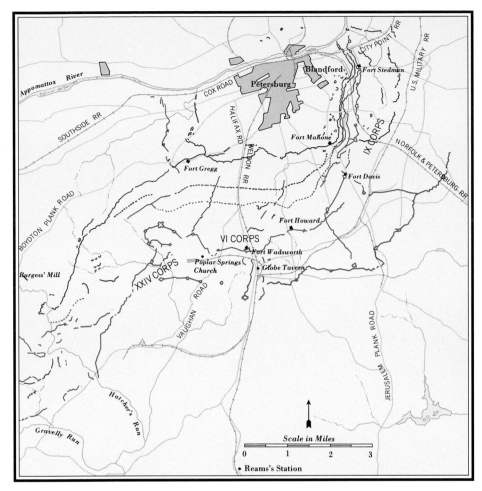

Galvanized by word of Sheridan's victory at Five Forks, Grant's forces at Petersburg launched a concentrated assault on the weakened Confederate defenses at dawn on April 2. Major General John Parke's IX Corps was initially unable to capture the Confederate strong point of Fort Mahone, but Major General Horatio Wright's VI Corps broke through the Confederate lines west of Petersburg, cutting the Boydton Plank Road and the Southside Railroad. By nightfall, Major General John Gibbon's XXIV Corps had taken Fort Gregg in heavy fighting, Fort Mahone had fallen and Lee had withdrawn to the innermost line of defense. He now had no choice but to evacuate Petersburg.

of double-shotted canister. Still they pressed on, tearing aside the abatis and pouring into the flooded ditch, where wounded men drowned in the mud and water. By 9 a.m. Brigadier General Robert Potter's division had managed to capture much of Fort Mahone and its surrounding trench lines; but Potter was unable to effect a breakthrough, and he fell wounded by a shot that tore into his stomach. The Confederate defenders were rallied by the heroic example of officers like Lieutenant Colonel John C. Goodgame of the 12th Alabama, who stood atop a traverse shouting "Alabamians! Stand up! Aim low and fire like men!" Soon, recalled a soldier of the 53rd North Carolina, "the open space inside of Fort Mahone was literally covered with blue-coated corpses."

It was a different story on the Confederate right, where the works were less formidable than at Fort Mahone. Advancing in a massive wedge, Wright's VI Corps brushed the

Confederate pickets aside and, despite heavy losses, managed to breach the entrenchments at several points simultaneously. The defenders fought hand to hand in a vain effort to stem the blue juggernaut. As Captain Charles Gould of the 5th Vermont leaped into the Confederate lines, he was bayoneted through the mouth and cheek. Gould sabered his assailant, but was slashed across the head by another artillerist and bayoneted in the back by a third soldier. A sergeant following Gould saved the captain's life by clubbing his musket butt across the head of one of Gould's attackers. All along VI Corps's front, Hazard Stevens reported, the Confederates were "swept away and scattered like chaff before a tornado."

Wild with the victory, Wright's men boiled onward, formation and discipline forgotten, over the Boydton Plank Road to the Southside Railroad a mile beyond. With difficulty, Wright got some of his men organized again, then swung to the left and swept down the Confederate line to Hatcher's Run. There his troops met John Gibbon's XXIV Corps, which had brushed aside the Confederate force in front of them. Gibbon now faced his corps around to begin the drive on Petersburg itself.

Word of the disastrous breakthrough did not at once reach General A. P. Hill at his headquarters west of the city. The previous evening, Hill had inspected his line and had gone to bed concerned about his ability to withstand an assault. He was awakened with the news that Gordon was heavily engaged on the left, at Fort Mahone; but he got no report from his own lines. Before daylight, Hill rode to Lee's headquarters a mile and a half away for a conference.

Pushing aside chevaux-de-frise, the 2nd Division of IX Corps storms Fort Mahone during the climactic Federal attack on the Confederate works around Petersburg. Colonel George W. Gowen (*left*) was leading the charge of the 48th Pennsylvania when he was hit in the face by a shell fragment and killed instantly.

Lee was weary and ill, lying in bed partially clothed, listening to the guns, suffering from what may have been an attack of rheumatism. Soon Longstreet arrived, in advance of the reinforcements he was bringing across the river. The three generals were discussing the bleak situation when an officer burst in to report that Hill's lines had been struck and broken and that Federal skirmishers were approaching.

The Federals were not skirmishers but small groups of VI Corps attackers who had lost touch with their regiments as they surged over the Confederate works. Still,

they were there; Lee could see them with his field glasses from his headquarters at the Turnbull house. General Hill mounted up, and with Colonel Charles Venable of Lee's staff and two couriers he raced to try to stem the breakthrough.

Federal soldiers were scattered over the countryside. Hill's party took two prisoners at pistol-point and sent them to the rear with one of the couriers. A few minutes later, Hill ordered Venable to deploy some Confederate artillery he had spotted on the Cox road. Next Hill headed west, crossed the Boydton Plank Road, then continued along it toward the southwest. "Sergeant," Hill said to G. W. Tucker, his remaining courier, "should anything happen to me you must go back to General Lee and report it."

Moments later the men spotted two Federals in the trees ahead. "We must take them," Hill snapped, drawing his revolver and riding ahead without hesitation. The bluecoats — Corporal John Mauk and Private Daniel Wolford of the 138th Pennsylvania — took cover and leveled their rifles.

"If you fire, you'll be swept to hell," shouted Tucker. "Our men are here — Surrender!" He was trying to keep ahead of Hill, who had closed to within 20 yards of the Federals. "Surrender!" shouted Hill, but the answer came as spitting lead. Wolford's bullet, meant for Tucker, went wild, but Corporal Mauk's shot pierced Hill's heart. He was dead before he hit the ground.

As ordered, Tucker rode back and reported to Lee, whose eyes filled with tears at the news. "He is at rest now," Lee murmured, "and we who are left are the ones to suffer."

The welcome change of a bright and sunny spring day went unnoticed as Lee reviewed his shattered army's irreparable situation.

What remained of Pickett's force was cut off and out of the fight. Anderson's corps had been sent to reinforce Pickett and could neither reach him nor return to the right flank. What remained of the right — Henry Heth's and Cadmus M. Wilcox's divisions of Hill's corps — in turn had been severed from the rest of the army by the wedge driven by VI Corps and had then retreated in confusion from their fortifications. Only Gordon, outnumbered 2 to 1, by shifting his men to each threatened point, was holding on the left.

With Sheridan nearing the Southside Railroad and the roads leading to the southwest, most of the Confederate forces at Petersburg would have to retreat northward, across the city's bridges over the Appomattox. Only then would they be able to head west. Getting through the bottleneck that the bridges presented was going to take time; somehow the advancing Federals had to be held off until nightfall. With the enemy threatening to overrun his headquarters, Lee prepared to move into Petersburg to organize a last stand, but first he sent a telegram to Secretary of War John C. Breckinridge: "I advise that all preparation be made for leaving Richmond tonight."

A messenger took a copy of the wire to President Davis, who on that Sunday morning was in his usual pew at St. Paul's Episcopal Church. After reading it, "Mr. Davis arose, and was noticed to walk rather unsteadily out of the church," one parishioner wrote later. His face, said another, "was set, so we could read nothing." But as more messengers arrived, and more officials hurriedly left the church, everyone understood. The minister ended the services and the anxious worshippers hurried to their homes.

Brigadier General John R. Cooke, mean-

while, had re-formed the remains of Heth's and Wilcox's divisions on a ridge near Sutherland Station, on the Southside Railroad two miles north of what had been the Confederate right flank. They were pursued by II Corps and barely had time to throw up breastworks before General Miles's division confronted them and attacked.

The Confederates — about 1,200 men — were determined and reasonably well entrenched, but the Federal soldiers, tasting triumph, launched a headlong assault. "They did not advance at even a moderate pace," wrote Captain James F. J. Caldwell of Samuel McGowan's South Carolina brigade, "nor even halt to dress their lines. But, with yells of mingled confidence and ferocity, they rushed forward rapidly, disordering their line and breaking through all control."

Confederate artillery blasted away, said Caldwell, "but so wild was their aim and so great the impetus of the enemy that the latter never staggered a moment, but pressed up

towards us." The two lines collided with a roar — both sides shouting, both firing, said Caldwell, "volley to volley." This time the Confederate musketry, "a perfect sheet of lead," prevailed. The Federals were rocked, and at last retreated. A second attack, at 12:30 p.m., was also repulsed.

Two hours later, Miles tried again, sending Colonel John Ramsey's brigade to flank the Confederate right while the other brigades charged the center. A curious thing happened as the Federals launched their third attack: The Southern soldiers began to argue about whether to continue the fight. "A wild uproar arose among us," Caldwell wrote. "Some were for resisting to the last, some advised immediate flight, some gave up the cause and counseled unconditional surrender."

Not surprisingly, Miles's third assault succeeded. The Confederate line collapsed from right to left, 600 men were captured, and the confused and disheartened survivors

Major John Gibbon's XXIV Corps attacks Fort Gregg on the inner defense line at Petersburg early in the afternoon on April 2. "Gregg raged like the crater of a volcano," wrote Captain William M. Owen (opposite) of the New Orleans Washington Artillery, "wreathing our flag as well in honor as in the smoke of death."

fell back toward the Appomattox. Caldwell called it the "most disorderly movement I ever saw among Confederate troops." For the rest of the day, he said, a "weary, mortified, angry stream of men poured through the fields and roads," making their way, in small groups and large, to the northwest along the river.

Robert E. Lee had moved his headquarters by then. The Turnbull house had been struck by an artillery shell while Lee was still in it — by the end of the day it would be burned to the ground — and cannon fire had followed him down the road as he departed.

Lee established a temporary headquarters in a house near Petersburg and began to plan his withdrawal. He worked with great care despite numerous interruptions. One was a dispatch from Jefferson Davis, in which the President complained that to depart from Richmond that night would necessitate "the loss of many valuables, both for the want of time to pack and of transportation." For an instant Lee's calm demeanor cracked. He ripped the message apart and said: "I am sure I gave him sufficient notice." But his answering message to Davis was as gracious as ever, saying only that he thought it "absolutely necessary that we should abandon our position tonight."

The plans for withdrawal were complicated. The army was spread over a wide area around Petersburg and Richmond, and various units would confront different problems in getting to an assembly point. That point — previously selected and made known to Lee's commanders — was the little town of Amelia Court House, about 35 miles west of Petersburg, on the Richmond & Danville Railroad. To avoid jamming the roads, several routes would have to be used. The Ap-

pomattox River, which ran southeastward between Amelia and Petersburg, would be a serious obstacle. Some of Lee's units would have to cross it twice — and of the three major bridges over the river, at least one was thought to be out.

But the army would never reach Amelia Court House unless the Federals were kept out of Petersburg until nightfall, when the Confederates would have a reasonable chance of getting across the river. There remained an inner line of strong fortifications from which to defend the city; these works stretched between the Boydton Plank Road and the river, scarcely a mile west of Petersburg. Longstreet's men were filing into the line as fast as they arrived. But the Federals — Ord's command and Wright's VI Corps, with Humphreys and most of II Corps not far behind — threatened to get there first.

At 1 p.m., Longstreet needed two more hours to get his men into position. But time had run out. General Grant was watching the action from a nearby hill, whittling and rapping out orders. He directed General Ord to attack the Confederate position, and Ord in turn allotted the responsibility to John Gibbon's XXIV Corps.

The duty of holding the crucial stretch of earthworks fell to General Cadmus M. Wilcox's division, and he gave the most critical assignment — the defense of the strong points known as Fort Gregg and Battery Whitworth — to a brigade of Mississippians commanded by Brigadier General Nathaniel Harris. The Confederates were outnumbered by more than 10 to 1, but no one flinched from the task. Inside Fort Gregg, Lieutenant Colonel James H. Duncan told the troops of the 12th and 16th Mississippi

A Confederate Hero's Posthumous Journey

An hour after he died in combat on April 2, the body of Lieutenant General Ambrose Powell Hill *(left)* was recovered, along with his cape, hat and sword *(below)*, by his provost guard. But there was neither time nor means to properly honor one of the Confederacy's ranking heroes.

At the request of Hill's wife, Dolly, his remains were taken to Richmond for burial. But by the time the ambulance arrived, Richmond was in flames and the bridges across the James were choked with fleeing soldiers and civilians. No undertaker was available, so Hill's relatives tended the body themselves and placed it in a cheap coffin they found in an abandoned furniture store. Transporting it through Federal lines to the Hills' home county of Culpeper, 100 miles north, was out of the question; they traveled instead to nearby Chesterfield County, where other family members had taken refuge. There Hill was buried in an unmarked grave.

Years later, the general's remains were returned to Richmond. In 1891 they found a final resting place in the foundation of a monument erected in his memory.

Regiments, "Men, the salvation of Lee's army is in your keeping." When the flag of the 48th Mississippi was shot from its staff at Battery Whitworth, General Harris tied the banner to a musket and climbed on top of the parapet, flaunting the banner at the Federals as they advanced.

Gibbon's leading division under Brigadier General Robert Foster was staggered by a hail of fire from the Confederate works. "Each defender had two or more rifles at hand," noted Private Frank Foote of the 48th Mississippi, "and while the rear rank loaded them, the front rank handled them with most deadly execution." Yet the attackers pressed on, tumbling into the ditch and battling their way up the steep parapet, using their bayonets and swords to dig footholds in the muddy soil. Brigadier General John W. Turner's division came piling in behind Foster's men, and soon a dozen Federal flags had been planted on the ramparts.

The fighting was as desperate as any the War had seen. Sergeant Albert Leach and another man from the 12th West Virginia were among the first on the parapet of Fort Gregg. When Leach's comrade was shot, the sergeant later wrote, he "rolled over against me, his brains flying all over me" and fell back into the ditch. When Leach shouted at the defenders to surrender, they yelled back, "You'll see us in hell first!" More Federals poured into the melee. "I could only parry thrusts and cuts from bayonets and sabres until almost exhausted," West Virginian Charles Reeder reported. "My determination then was to sell my life as dearly as possible, and I clubbed right and left." Lieutenant Colonel Thomas Wildes of the 116th Ohio leaped into Fort Gregg beside a Confederate captain who cried out: "Never surrender to the damned Yankees!" Two of Wildes's men beat him to death.

The defenders of Battery Whitworth and Fort Gregg were submerged beneath a flood of men in blue. "The sight was truly terrific," an officer of the 39th Illinois recalled. "Dead men and the dying lay strewn all about, and it was with the greatest difficulty that we could prevent our infuriated soldiers from shooting down and braining all who survived of the stubborn foe." Of the 214 Confederates in Fort Gregg, only 30 were still standing; 55 had been killed and 129 wounded. The loss in Battery Whitworth was nearly as great. Gibbon's attackers had also paid a heavy price: 714 men killed, wounded or missing.

The valiant Confederate defense of Fort Gregg gave Lee the time he needed to deploy General Longstreet's troops behind the innermost line of earthworks protecting Petersburg. Ord and Wright, reluctant to launch a further assault, were content to rest on their hard-won laurels. To the east, Fort Mahone had finally fallen to IX Corps, but there also the Federals foundered against Lee's final line of defense.

Still, the survival of Petersburg was measured in hours, and after 10 months of slaughter, that in itself was enough for the Federal soldiers. "Our flags were floating on the Rebel works," wrote Private William Hopkins of the 7th Rhode Island Infantry Regiment. "And, as daylight faded into darkness, we hopefully watched them, clinging closer and closer to their eagle-peaked staffs until they were lost in the gloom. Thus closed that wild, stormy Sabbath, a day of blood, carnage, and victory."

Ever since the disruption of the Sunday service at St. Paul's Church that morning,

according to Confederate Captain Clement Sulivane, "a strange agitation was perceptible on the streets of Richmond." Everyone understood the city was about to be abandoned to the Federals. In fact, preparations had been under way for more than a month, and most civilian officials below Cabinet rank had already left. Yet there was still

shock; this was, after all, the capital of the Confederacy, where citizens had felt, as Sulivane put it, "a singular security."

Jefferson Davis and members of the Cabinet, the Archives and the Treasury were soon on their way to Danville. "All that Sabbath day," remembered Sulivane, "the trains came and went, wagons, vehicles and

A cavalry escort leads the carriages of Confederate officials fleeing Richmond across the James River on the night of April 2. "The waters sparkled and rushed on by the burning city," recalled a soldier who had guarded the bridge. "Every now and then, as a magazine exploded, a column of white smoke rose up, instantaneously followed by a deafening sound."

horsemen rumbled and dashed to and fro." That evening the Confederates set fire to Richmond's warehouses — over the objections of the city fathers — to keep the valuable contents from falling into the hands of the Federals. The fires quickly spread.

With the departure of the civil authorities, the streets of Richmond were taken over by a rowdy and menacing mob — thugs, thieves, prostitutes, Army deserters and convicts who had broken out of the penitentiary. There was virtually no one available to control either the fires or the crowds; the municipal police and firefighters were few and inadequate. To make matters worse, orders had been given for the destruction of the city's liquor supplies, and casks had been emptied into the gutters, where rough-looking people immediately began scooping up the whiskey in buckets and pitchers. Others began breaking into shops.

"It was an extraordinary night," recalled newspaper editor Edward A. Pollard; "disorder, pillage, shouts, mad revelry of confusion." Mobs could be seen in the flickering firelight, "besieging the commissary stores, destroying liquor, intent perhaps upon pillage, and swaying to and fro in whatever momentary passion possessed them." As the hours passed, said Pollard, "the sidewalks were encumbered with broken glass; stores were entered at pleasure and stripped from top to bottom; yells of drunken men, shouts of roving pillagers, wild cries of distress filled the air and made the night hideous." It was, said Mrs. George Pickett, who was living in Richmond, a "saturnalia."

All the while, Lee's army was streaming northward across the Appomattox from Petersburg, southward across the James below Richmond, then westward toward Amelia Court House. Around midnight the Heavy Artillerymen manning the James River defenses at Chaffin's and Drewry's Bluffs abandoned their positions, destroying the ordnance that could not be removed. The sailors of the fleet joined in the withdrawal, scuttling their vessels behind them. "The explosions began just as we got across the river," wrote Artillery Major Robert Stiles. "As the ironclads exploded, it seemed as if the very dome of heaven would be shattered down upon us."

Captain Sulivane, in command of 200 local militia, was posted at the only remaining bridge across the James at Richmond, with orders to burn it after the last Confederate soldiers were across. From there he watched the "terrible splendor" of Richmond dying.

At dawn, while Sulivane was anxiously watching the Federal horsemen entering the city, a Confederate ambulance train forced its way through the mobs thronging the commissary depot on the Richmond waterfront and crossed the bridge. It was followed by a brigade of cavalry commanded by Brigadier General Martin W. Gary. After the long column had thundered over the bridge, Gary continued to sit his horse nearby while the long minutes passed; Sulivane fretted, his kerosene, tar and pine logs ready to be ignited. Then another company of cavalry appeared, dashing for the bridge with blueclad riders not far behind. "My rear-guard," General Gary explained. The last Confederate defenders of Richmond galloped across the bridge and away.

Gary touched his hat and rode after them. "All over, good-by," he shouted to Sulivane. "Blow her to hell."

The Fallen at Fort Mahone

"It is probable that never since the invention of gunpowder has such a cannonade taken place," declared the Federal officer in charge of the climactic April 2 bombardment of the defenses of Petersburg. On the morning after that holocaustic assault, a photographer named Thomas Roche carried his bulky equipment to a captured strong point in the Confederate line, which had defied Grant's army for 10 desperate months. Known as Fort Mahone, the earthworks had been manned by troops of the 53rd North Carolina. Roche found the place defended now only by Confederate dead; he photographed these men sprawled as they had fallen, in Fort Mahone's mud-choked labyrinth of trenches. Some were clearly veterans, but many were boys—one only 14 years old, by Roche's estimate. Their faces evince a repose that contrasts poignantly with their torn bodies. The deaths Roche recorded, including the picture opposite and those on the following pages, seem all the more painful because the victims were struck down in one of the War's last battles—for a cause already lost.

A Race for Survival

"Flankers and scouting parties of cavalry were constantly bringing in scores of prisoners from the woods on either side. They were lost from the main body of their army; they were hungry and tired; and if there was a Confederacy to sustain, they could not find it in the woods."

LIEUTENANT COLONEL FREDERIC C. NEWHALL OF SHERIDAN'S STAFF

Mrs. Phoebe Yates Pember of Richmond was looking toward the rising sun on the morning of April 3 when "a single Federal bluejacket rose above the hill." Soon, she said, "another and another sprang up as if out of the earth, but still all remained quiet. About seven o'clock there fell upon the ears the steady clatter of horses' hoofs, and winding around Rocketts, close under Chimborazo Hill, came a small and compact body of Federal cavalrymen. They were well mounted, well accoutered, well fed — a rare sight in Southern streets — the advance of that vaunted army that for four years had so hopelessly knocked at the gates of the Southern Confederacy."

It had fallen to Major General Godfrey Weitzel, whose XXV Corps in the lines north of the James River had sat out the momentous fighting of the past five days, to take possession of Richmond and raise over it the flag of the United States. This was a heavy irony, since Weitzel's command included all the black troops formerly assigned to both the Army of the James and IX Corps of the Army of the Potomac.

Weitzel's foot soldiers followed the cavalry into Richmond, stacked their arms in Capitol Square and went to work to control the fires still raging throughout the city. Every able-bodied man the Federals found on the streets — black, white, straggler or convict — was required to help. "In this manner," wrote one of Weitzel's aides, "the fire was extinguished and perfect order restored in an incredibly short time."

By all accounts, the behavior of the Federal soldiers was exemplary. They were firm but kindly in their treatment of the conquered citizenry, doing their best to reassure the women, distribute food to the needy and protect the helpless. One officer responded to the appeal of a frantic young woman who said her bedridden mother could not flee the approaching flames. Entering the house, he found the invalid to be the wife of Robert E. Lee. The officer posted guards at the house and made an ambulance available to evacuate Mrs. Lee if necessary.

Still, the troops filling the streets of Richmond were the enemy, and their presence evoked a conflict in Southern hearts that was reflected with precision in the diary of 14-year-old Frances Hunt. "The Yankees are behaving very well," she observed, "considering it is them."

That same morning, the Federals — General Grant among them — had marched into Petersburg. The streets along the riverfront were still crowded with Confederate soldiers struggling to get away, and Grant could have wreaked terrible damage with his cannon. But he let the stragglers go. "I had not the heart," he explained later, "to turn the artillery upon such a mass of defeated and fleeing men." Besides, he added, "I hoped to capture them soon."

Abraham Lincoln had been at City Point

This handmade identification tag, a lead disk on a brass chain, was worn by Private Samuel Eddy of Company D, 37th Massachusetts, in the savage fighting at Sayler's Creek. Severely wounded by a bayonet thrust, Eddy was able to walk to the rear and get medical help, but he lost the tag. It was found on the site more than a century later.

throughout the past week, keeping abreast of the stirring events by means of dispatches from Grant. When Petersburg fell, Lincoln hurried there for a brief, triumphant meeting with his general in chief; the next day he decided to visit Richmond.

Accompanied by his 12-year-old son, Tad, and by Rear Admiral David Porter, Lincoln stepped ashore unannounced in a remote part of the conquered enemy capital that Weitzel's force had not yet occupied. The boat that was carrying the President's escort of Marines had run aground, and he was protected by no more than a dozen sailors armed with carbines.

The only people on hand to observe the historic arrival were some black laborers working nearby. In an instant they recognized the visitor, dropped their spades and clustered around the President. Some of them fell to their knees and kissed his feet while Lincoln helplessly protested. More former slaves materialized. "They seemed to spring from the earth," Admiral Porter recalled. "They came, tumbling and shouting, from over the hills and from the waterside, where no one was seen as we had passed." The alarmed sailors formed a cordon around Lincoln and fixed their bayonets as the crowd, said Porter, "poured in so fearfully that I thought we all stood a chance of being crushed to death."

At length, Lincoln said a few words to the jubilant mob: "You are free," he told them, "free as air." Slowly the little party moved on, accompanied by the burgeoning crowd. It was a warm day, and Lincoln was beginning to look dusty and hot. At last Porter spotted a Federal cavalryman — the first occupation soldier he had seen since landing — and sent the man in search of an escort.

Twenty minutes later a troop of riders appeared and managed to push back the crowd, allowing Lincoln to proceed safely. After a walk of about two miles, Lincoln arrived at General Weitzel's headquarters, in Jefferson Davis' former executive mansion. One of the President's party said Lincoln was "pale and haggard, utterly worn out," but a drink of water revived him and he went on a tour of the house, showing a boyish pleasure at the opportunity to look over Davis' living quarters.

Later that afternoon, Lincoln visited other parts of the city, riding in a carriage and attended by a cavalry escort. He saw the infamous Libby Prison and the Confederate capitol and had an evening meeting with Judge John A. Campbell, who had participated in the recent Hampton Roads peace conference.

Few details survive of Lincoln's activities in Richmond that day, but there is a report from Mrs. George Pickett, the comely young wife of the Confederate general. Answering her door, she found "a tall, gaunt, sad-faced man in ill-fitting clothes standing outside." He said: "I am Abraham Lincoln." When she gasped, "The President!" he said, "No; Abraham Lincoln, George's old friend." Lincoln and Pickett had known each other before the War.

Mrs. Pickett was holding her 10-month-old son, and Lincoln took the infant in his arms and accepted a damp kiss. As he handed back the child before leaving, Lincoln said to him: "Tell your father that I forgive him for the sake of your bright eyes."

While Lincoln visited Richmond, the vanguard of the Army of Northern Virginia arrived in the pretty red-brick town of Amelia Court House. All day long, the scattered

Confederate units struggled to reconcentrate there. Longstreet's corps, accompanied by what remained of A. P. Hill's corps, under Henry Heth, was the first to arrive, having marched northwest from Petersburg. Gordon's corps was close behind. Before long they were joined by Mahone's division. Richard Ewell was marching the forces that had defended Richmond toward Amelia by a more northerly road, and south of the James the remains of Pickett's division, Anderson's corps and Fitzhugh Lee's cavalry found that after their defeat at Five Forks they had the shortest march of all.

Sheridan's cavalry was close on Fitzhugh Lee's heels, and the Virginian had to turn and fight twice on April 3. At Namozine Church, Custer's leading brigade under Colonel William Wells attacked Lee's rear guard, Brigadier General Rufus Barringer's brigade, inflicting heavy casualties. By the next morning Sheridan was certain that the Confederates were concentrating their forces at Amelia Court House. He also understood that the race was not for that place, but for the vital railroad junction near Burkeville, 15 miles southwest of Amelia. If Lee's army could get there ahead of the Federals, it might still escape to join Johnston's army. Sheridan ordered George Crook's division to strike for Jetersville, a station halfway between Amelia and Burkeville. Charles Griffin was to follow with V Corps.

Thus instead of pursuing the Confederates, the Federals raced alongside them, trying to get ahead of Lee and bring him to bay. Sheridan's route led toward Amelia — and George Meade, riding with his army although seriously ill, sent both II and VI Corps marching westward in the cavalry's wake. Their course was a full 20 miles shorter than the 55-mile arc some of the Confederate troops had to travel. The Federals, in fact, seemed to have all the advantages — superior numbers, plenty of food and ammunition, and the fiery exhilaration of victory.

The Confederates were in far worse physical shape, but they were running for their lives, for the survival of the Confederacy and for General Lee. Despite their privations, some of them were ebullient, "like schoolboys on a holiday," a sergeant said. They were out of the trenches at last and back on the road. They had been told there would be plenty to eat at Amelia, the sun was shining and they could hope again.

But the lift to Confederate spirits could not overcome for long the twin enemies of hunger and exhaustion. By the second day, many soldiers were sleeping as they walked. When there was a halt, the men would drop to the ground until the march resumed. Then, when another soldier tripped over them, they would lurch to their feet and stumble on.

Pickett's force had been "so crushed by the defeats of the last few days that it straggled along without strength and almost without thought," said Lieutenant James F. J. Caldwell of the 1st South Carolina. "There were not many words spoken. An indescribable sadness weighed upon us."

For a time the marchers included clusters of fleeing civilians. "There were citizens in broadcloth," recalled Lieutenant Colonel William W. Blackford, "politicians, members of Congress, prominent citizens, almost all on foot, but sometimes there were wagons and carriages loaded with them. Some ladies too might be seen occasionally and generally they were calmer than the men."

Among Ewell's troops was a group of

Lieutenant Johnston L. DePeyster of the 13th New York Heavy Artillery, assisted by Captain Loomis L. Langdon of the 1st U.S. Artillery, raises the U.S. flag over the Confederate capitol on the morning of April 3. Before leaving the roof, the two officers drank a toast; DePeyster later reenacted his feat for a photographer (*far right*).

Navy men — sailors and Marines who had been assigned to the ironclads and gunboats on the James River. Their ships were gone, but they had formed a battalion of infantry under Commodore John R. Tucker and were tramping along in their strange uniforms, responding to such outlandish commands as "To starboard, march!"

There was also a large contingent of former noncombatants — "a perfect army of bureau clerks, quartermasters, commissaries and ordnance officers," continued Colonel Blackford, "all dressed in fine clothes and uniforms, with white faces, scared half to death, fellows who for the most part had been in bomb-proof offices ever since the War began and who did not relish the prospect of smelling powder now." Many of

them had been organized into independent companies known as the Richmond Locals and had been placed in Brigadier General Seth Barton's brigade. The Locals, along with the Naval Battalion, were now serving under the command of Robert E. Lee's eldest son, Custis Lee.

As they moved westward over five separate routes, the varied units of the Army of Northern Virginia were accompanied by hundreds of wagons, ambulances and artillery pieces in cumbersome trains. All of the marchers — whatever their previous service or the state of their morale — were buoyed by a single prospect: that of eating their fill at Amelia Court House.

During the final days of the siege, Lee had asked the Confederate Commissary Department to collect a substantial store of food in Richmond. This had been done; 350,000 rations had been gathered in the capital, and Lee wanted them sent ahead to Amelia. Another 500,000 rations of bread and 1.5 million rations of meat had been collected at Danville; as a result, Lee had every reason to believe that, for now at least, his supply worries were over.

But when Lee looked for the rations, upon his arrival at Amelia Court House, he made an appalling discovery. He found an abundant cache of artillery caissons, ammunition and harness — but not a single ration of food. For a moment, according to an officer standing nearby, the discovery "completely paralyzed" the imperturbable Lee. "An anxious and haggard expression came to his face."

The army continued to converge on the rendezvous, camping in the streets and overflowing into the surrounding countryside. Soon thousands of hungry men were jammed into the little town and its environs and additional commands were waiting beyond the Appomattox. Not a bit of food was available for them, and no one knew why.

Blame for the confusion was hurled in several directions. Some insisted that the necessary railroad cars were not available because they had been commandeered to save what staff officer John Esten Cooke described as "the rubbish of the departments." Jefferson Davis indignantly denied this. The simple fact seems to have been that in the haste of moving out of the Turnbull house, Lee's headquarters staff had failed to get word to the Commissary officials that Lee was counting on the supplies to be waiting for him at Amelia Court House.

In desperation, Lee pulled some wagons and teams out of the trains parked around the town and addressed a plea to the citizens of Amelia County. "The Army of Northern Virginia arrived here today, expecting to find plenty of provisions," Lee wrote. "But to my surprise and regret, I find not a pound of subsistence for man or horse. I must therefore appeal to your generosity and charity to supply as far as each one is able the wants of the brave soldiers who have battled for your liberty for four years."

Lee armed his quartermasters with this message and sent them out into a countryside that had been combed repeatedly for food, with orders to try one more time. Until they returned, the army could not move. The slim but precious lead over the pursuing Federal infantry would have to be sacrificed.

While the foragers were out, Lee reorganized his wagon trains, directing all but the most critically needed wagons to follow a circuitous route to the north, keeping the Confederate army between them and the Federals. He also ordered the destruction of the excess artillery rounds stockpiled at Amelia; only enough ammunition to fill the artillery's limber chests was set aside. The ear-shattering detonations caused an incident that demonstrated the fragility of the army's self-control.

Private Carlton McCarthy and his fellow artillerists were sitting around chatting quietly, "when suddenly the earth shook with a tremendous explosion and an immense column of smoke rushed up into the air to a great height. For a moment there was the greatest consternation, while regiments broke and fled in wildest confusion." McCarthy's unit, which had been assigned to protect their battalion's flank, leaped up and prepared to do battle. Only then did the

A Presidential Favor That Backfired

The North Carolina regiments commanded by Brigadier General Rufus Barringer (*right*) had fought valiantly at Five Forks, and on April 3 they were struggling to reach Amelia Court House, where Lee's army was reassembling. But at Namozine Church, still almost 25 miles from their destination, the 800 Confederates ran into a Union force ten times their size and had to fight again. For Barringer, the engagement would initiate a curious misadventure.

As his men were about to be overwhelmed, Barringer led them to apparent refuge in some woods. But while exploring the area, Barringer by his own account "was deceived by a squad of Sheridan's scouts in Confederate uniforms" and taken prisoner. His subsequent transfer to Federal headquarters at City Point happened to coincide with a visit by Abraham Lincoln. The President, who said he "had never seen a live Rebel general," asked to be introduced to the prisoner.

"There was a Barringer in Congress with me," remembered Lincoln, "and from your state too."

Replied the general, "That was my brother, Sir."

Pleased to recall less troubled times, Lincoln reminisced at length about his friend. When their talk ended, Lincoln's sympathy for Barringer's predicament, and perhaps his loyalty to an old comrade, prompted him to ask, "Do you think I could be of any service to you?"

Barringer replied frankly, "If anyone could be of service to a poor devil in my situation, I presume you are the man."

So Lincoln wrote a note to Secretary of War Stanton, requesting that Barringer's detention in Washington be "as comfortable as possible under the circumstances."

Unfortunately, the President's kind gesture backfired. By the time Stanton received the message, Lincoln had been assassinated; in the tense atmosphere of the moment, the note brought Barringer under suspicion. His captors interrogated him again and again about his encounter with the late President.

BRIGADIER GENERAL RUFUS BARRINGER

Not until late July of 1865, months after most other Confederate prisoners had been freed, was the hapless general finally released.

---

abashed soldiers discover that their commanders were merely exploding unneeded ammunition. "Then what laughter and hilarity prevailed," McCarthy recorded, "among these famishing men!"

The foragers returned during the morning of April 5, but their wagons were virtually empty. The local farmers had been stripped clean the previous winter. In McCarthy's battalion each man was issued two ears of corn that had been intended for the horses. The corn was parched in the campfires and eaten later; it was so hard, said McCarthy, that "it made the jaws ache and the gums and teeth so sore as to cause almost unendurable pain." A number of men wandered off to look for food on their own. Some of these strays returned, some did not.

The absence of food made it even more imperative that the Confederate push westward resume immediately. "I know that the men and animals are much exhausted," noted Lee in a message to General Gordon. "But it is necessary to tax their strength." The soldiers understood their predicament. As Colonel William M. Owen, commanding the Washington Artillery of New Orleans, wrote in his diary, "It is now a race for life or death."

The Federal troops were equally aware of what was at stake. They outran their own wagon trains, "so elated by the reflection that at last they were following up a victory to its end," said Grant, "that they preferred marching without rations to running a possible risk of letting the enemy elude them." Private John Haley of the 17th Maine wrote in his journal, "We are jubilant. We have them on the run and victory is in the air."

Crook's cavalry and Griffin's V Corps had reached Jetersville, directly in Lee's path, on the afternoon of April 4. During the next 24 hours, Humphreys arrived with II Corps and Wright approached with VI Corps. General Meade intended to attack Lee at Amelia, of course, but to Sheridan's distress, he planned to wait until the morning of April 6, when Wright would be in position.

Sheridan did not want to wait. His patrols reported that Lee's wagon trains were already pulling out of Amelia Court House; Brigadier General Henry E. Davies' troopers had found and destroyed 180 Confederate wagons and had captured five artillery pieces at Painesville, a crossroads seven miles northwest of Amelia. Moreover, Sheridan did not want the Federal infantry to strike Lee in such a way that the Confederates could take to their heels again; he wanted to get in front and block them. Sheridan could not overrule Meade, but he knew who could; he sent an urgent message to Grant, who was farther south and heading directly to Burkeville with General Ord's command. "I wish you were here yourself," Sheridan said. "I feel confident of capturing the Army of Northern Virginia if we exert ourselves."

Grant, heeding Sheridan's appeal, hurried to Jetersville. He arrived late at night after a four-hour ride through dangerous country with only a small escort to protect him. Grant went over the situation with Meade and was not happy about it. But, beyond directing Ord's two corps to push on to Burkeville before going into bivouac, he could do nothing until dawn. Meade asked for and received the return of Griffin's V Corps to his command. Disgruntled, Sheridan moved his cavalry off to the left at first light while Meade advanced firmly — in the wrong direction.

When the Army of Northern Virginia resumed its march, leaving Amelia at midday on April 5, Lee knew that the Federal cavalry was at Jetersville. His men had captured two Federal scouts bearing important dis-

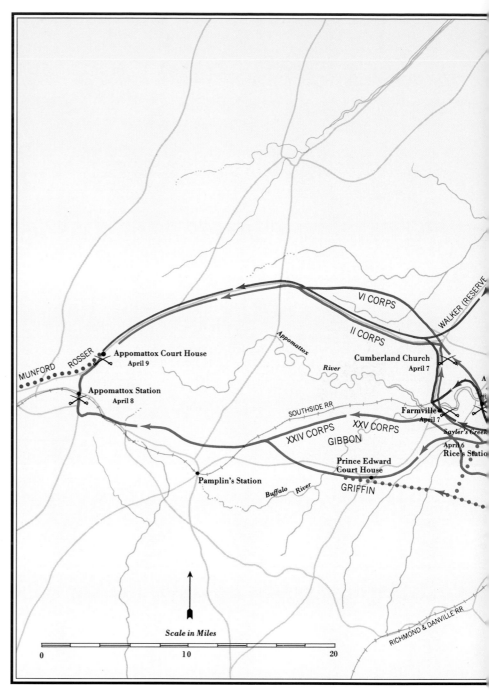

patches that revealed the Federal positions. Cavalry might have been brushed aside, but when Lee's riders had probed the Federal position at Jetersville they found infantry there as well, the vanguard of the hard-marching V Corps. Lee knew that if he attempted to smash through, Grant's mighty army would certainly overwhelm his depleted forces. He had to try to get around the Federals, not only to continue his escape but to go far enough down the railroad to get

After evacuating Richmond and Petersburg on April 2, Lee gathered his forces at Amelia Court House, planning to turn south and join Johnston in North Carolina. Grant hurled his armies in pursuit, sending Sheridan's cavalry to block Lee's line of march until the infantry could bring the Confederates to battle. Amid constant fighting, Lee eluded Grant but was always forced farther west. After severe clashes on April 6 and 7, at Sayler's Creek and around Farmville, Lee turned toward Lynchburg only to find his way blocked at Appomattox.

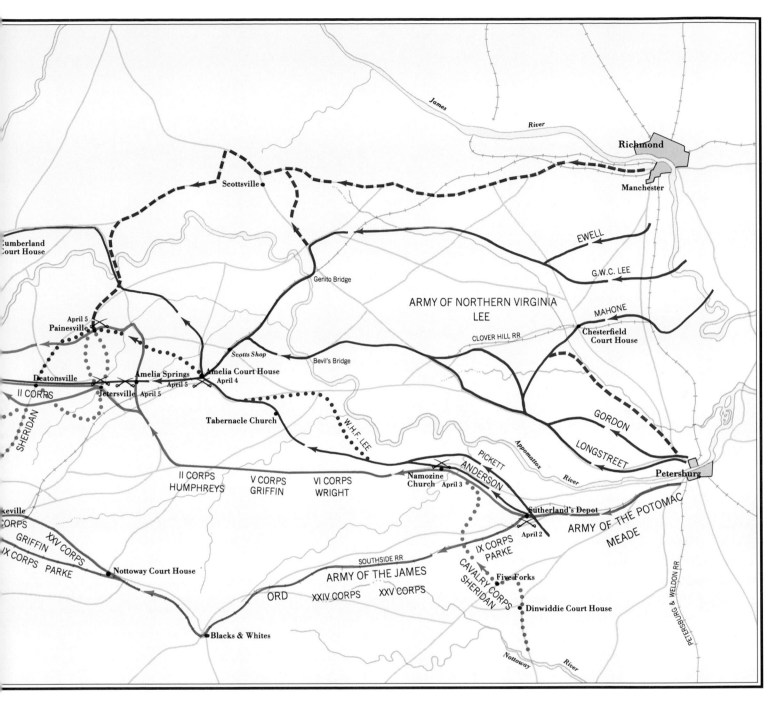

supplies. His men must have food, and soon.

Accordingly, Lee led his column on a swing to the north, around the Federal position. His route of march would pass through Rice's Station on the Southside Railroad, seven miles northwest of Burkeville. Once there he could receive food by rail from Lynchburg, then march west to that city or, preferably, head south until he again struck the Danville route — the way to Johnston's army. But with the Federal V Corps at Je-

tersville, and with II and VI Corps closing in fast, he would have to hurry.

The Army of Northern Virginia marched all afternoon on April 5, and then through the night, in heavy rain. The starving and exhausted soldiers stumbled forward, many losing all track of time and unable to remember afterward where they had been or what they had done. Some wandered away from the columns in search of food; others fell by the roadside. Captain McHenry Howard of

Custis Lee's staff recalled, "Every expedient was resorted to in order to obtain something to eat, however scanty, with total disregard of the ordinary rules of discipline and respect for private property."

General Davies' attack on the wagon train at Painesville had left the route blocked with wreckage; the surviving vehicles returned to the same roads being used by the infantry, adding to the congestion and slowing the march even more. Horses and mules broke down, forcing the abandonment of scores of wagons that carried the army's remaining scraps of food. "We stopped for what was supposed to be the midday meal," one officer recalled. "The midday was there, but the meal was not."

The Federals found the roads littered with discarded weapons, blanket rolls and artillery pieces in the wake of the fleeing army. Chalked on the side of one abandoned wagon was the message: "Weuns have found the last ditch." Most of the wagons still contained their cargo, and the Union soldiers picking through the wreckage were surprised at the variety of heavy, useless equipment the Confederates were carting along. "Cooking utensils, frying pans, stewpans, kettles, were plentiful," said Brigadier General Philip de Trobriand. "When a ship threatens to founder, they throw the freight into the sea," he added. "Lee's army refused to lighten itself in this way and was engulfed with its cargo."

The roads were filled with human flotsam as well — stragglers, deserters and men who simply could no longer stay awake. "Prisoners were pouring into our lines by the thou-

Crook's Federal cavalry, fighting dismounted (left) and on horseback (right), capture the men and guns escorting the main Confederate supply train near Painesville on April 5. The Federals seized and burned 180 wagons, destroying many of Lee's official papers in the process.

sands," said Private Theodore Gerrish of the 20th Maine. One cavalryman descended on a dirt-smudged Confederate who was cooling his feet in a stream while he mended his coat and called on him to surrender, shouting: "I've got you this time!"

The ragged Southerner did not look up from his needlework. "Yes," he said sourly. "You've got me, and a hell of a git you got!"

About this time a Confederate soldier encountered a straggler from General Longstreet's corps and heard him lament: "My shoes are gone; my clothes are almost gone. I'm weary, I'm sick, I'm hungry. My family have been killed or scattered. I have suffered all this for my country. I love my country. I would die — yes, I would die willingly because I love my country. But if this war is ever over, I'll be damned if I ever love another country!"

During the night a horse that had been tied to a fence broke away and stampeded along the column, dragging a piece of rail. The dazed Confederates, sure they were being attacked, panicked and started shooting. Fellow marchers returned the fire, and before sanity could be restored, several men had been killed or wounded. There were real attacks, as well; Sheridan's cavalrymen pounced time and again from parallel roads to the south of the Confederates.

Longstreet, urged on by Lee, led the melancholy march with his own and Heth's corps, followed by their wagons. Longstreet's vanguard was screened by Rooney Lee's cavalry. Next came Anderson's small corps and Ewell's Richmond garrison, reduced by straggling to fewer than 3,000 men — half its strength of three days earlier. Then came the rest of the army's trains, followed by Gordon's corps, still bringing up

the rear. It was supposed to be a forced march, but the pace was more like a crawl. The collapse of a small bridge over Flat Creek, on the Amelia Springs road, halted the artillery and trains until the engineers could be brought up to repair it. That night the army advanced only seven miles.

At sunrise on the 6th of April, Longstreet's van was little more than five miles from Rice's Station, but Gordon's rear guard was just leaving Amelia Springs, a hamlet four miles west of Amelia Court House. Thus when Meade launched his belated attack northeastward, General Humphreys, on the Federal left, reported "a strong column of the enemy's infantry" marching away to the west.

The Federal army halted, and when more reports confirmed that it was indeed heading away from the enemy, the men were faced about and took up the chase again, with Humphreys' II Corps in the lead. "A sharp running fight commenced at once with Gordon's corps," Humphreys recalled, "which was continued over a distance of fourteen miles, during which several partially entrenched positions were carried."

Gordon noted that "the roads and fields and woods swarmed with eager pursuers" and that his command was "in almost incessant battle." Despite their wretched condition, the Southern soldiers fought fiercely. "There was as much gallantry displayed by some of the Confederates in these little engagements," said Grant later, "as was displayed at any time during the War." During this hectic chase, II Corps got so far in front of the rest of the Federal army that Grant feared Lee's entire force might suddenly turn and overwhelm it.

When Longstreet, at the head of the army,

reached Rice's Station at midmorning on the 6th, he learned that several hundred Federals had just passed through, heading north along the railroad. The news was alarming; the reported enemy force was not large enough to attack the army, but it was certainly large enough to destroy the vital bridges across the Appomattox River, three miles to the north.

There the eastward-flowing river and the railroad — headed west for Lynchburg — intertwined. About four miles northeast of the market town of Farmville, the tracks crossed to the north side of the river by way of the so-called High Bridge, which spanned a flood plain half a mile wide at the dizzying height of 126 feet. Loss of this bridge and of the less-imposing wagon bridge beside it would cut one of the Confederates' few remaining lines of retreat.

Troops of General Ord's Army of the James — one division of Weitzel's XXV Corps and two divisions of Major General John Gibbon's XXIV Corps — had marched directly to Burkeville while the Army of the Potomac was veering north to Jetersville. Early on the morning of the 6th, Ord had dispatched nearly 900 men — the 123rd Ohio and the 54th Pennsylvania and three companies of his headquarters guard, the 4th Massachusetts Cavalry under Colonel Francis Washburn — to destroy the bridges.

The force was well past Rice's Station when the Confederates arrived there and learned of the threat. Longstreet rounded up all the cavalry he could find to give chase, telling General Thomas Rosser to take his division and destroy the Federals if it took the last man of his command to do it. Longstreet soon added General Thomas Munford's division to the force, giving Rosser a total of 1,200 horsemen. Word reached Ord that the Confederate cavalry was in pursuit and he dispatched his adjutant general, Colonel Theodore Read, to warn Washburn. After a brief discussion, the two officers decid-

Officers of the 2nd Rhode Island gather behind their colonel, Elisha H. Rhodes (*seated at left*). Just before the fighting started at Sayler's Creek, Captain Charles W. Gleason, the tall officer at center, said to Rhodes, "This will be the last battle if we win, and then you and I can go home." Within moments, Gleason was shot in the head and killed.

ed that they would continue their mission.

When Rosser's leading brigades caught up with the Federals around noon, the 80-man cavalry squadron had just driven a detachment of home guards away from the High Bridge. The Federal infantry waited on a hill near the Watson farmhouse, about half a mile to the south. Before Colonel Washburn could destroy the bridge, he heard firing behind him and galloped back to find his infantry support being attacked by three brigades of Confederates. Munford had dismounted his division and sent the men directly toward the Federal line while Rosser took his two brigades to the left behind a screen of trees to strike the Federals' flank.

On the afternoon of April 6, Federal cavalry under Merritt halted the advance of Anderson's corps on Rice's Station, three miles to the southwest. Ewell formed behind Little Sayler's Creek to face Wright's pursuing VI Corps. After a heavy bombardment, VI Corps divisions led by Seymour and Wheaton attacked across the shallow creek. Despite a brief check in the center, the brigades of Hamblin and Keifer enveloped the Confederate battle line, routing Ewell's men. At the same time, Merritt's cavalry, after several unsuccessful attempts, broke Anderson's line. Hundreds of Confederate soldiers surrendered near the Marshall farm.

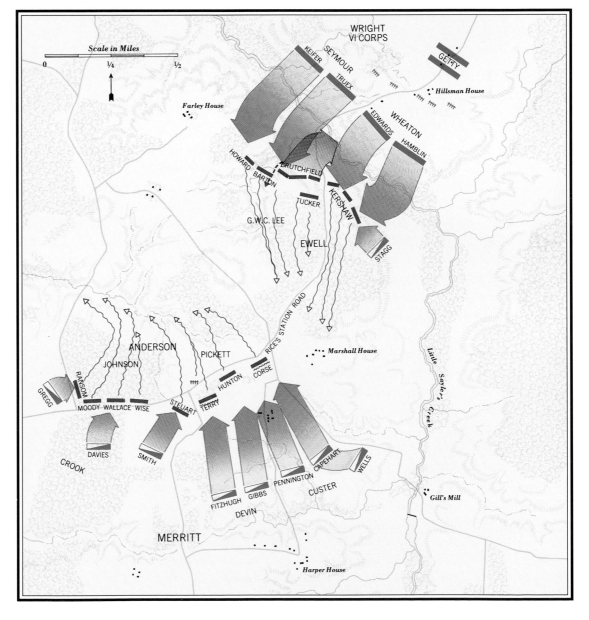

After another quick conference with Colonel Read, Washburn — unaware that he was facing two Confederate divisions — led a ferocious charge against the dismounted attackers in his front. At first the unexpected charge dismayed Munford's men and they were driven back; a Federal major, Edward T. Bouvé, recalled that Washburn's men "crashed through three lines of advancing enemies, tearing their formation asunder as the tornado cuts its way through the forest." But Rosser's brigades rode rapidly to assist their comrades. Despite the large force arrayed against him, Washburn continued his charge into the oncoming Confederates.

The fight dissolved into a swirling hand-to-hand struggle.

Confederate Brigadier General James Dearing and Washburn dashed by each other, exchanging saber cuts as they passed. Seconds later, a Confederate trooper shot Washburn through the cheek, tumbling him from his horse. Washburn was then struck in the head by a saber and mortally wounded. Dearing spotted Colonel Read and shot him dead. Then Dearing too was shot down. Within a few minutes the 4th Massachusetts was overwhelmed. All 11 of its officers, including its three company commanders, were casualties. Only seven enlisted men had been killed or wounded, but more than 60 were taken prisoner.

Once the Federal horsemen had been dealt with, the Confederates turned on the infantry, which had held its position on the hill instead of coming to the aid of the beleaguered 4th Massachusetts. Brigadier General John McCausland of Rosser's division ordered the 6th Virginia Cavalry and the 35th Virginia Cavalry Battalion to charge the Federal position. Colonel Reuben Boston of the 6th Virginia was killed in the attack, but his men drove the Federals from the hill. When the 35th Virginia rode around the flank of the fugitives, they surrendered en masse. The Confederates took nearly 800 men prisoner along with six colors and guidons and a complete brass band.

The Appomattox bridges remained in Confederate hands for the time being, but a Federal colonel who was being led away a prisoner told his captors jauntily, "Never mind, boys, Old Grant is after you. You will be in our predicament in 48 hours."

As the day wore on, Lee and Longstreet waited impatiently at Rice's Station for the rest of the Confederate army, which was struggling to close up. Grant recalled later that the iron-willed Lee "never permitted the head of his columns to stop because of any fighting that was going on in the rear." One result of this policy, Grant later wrote, was that Lee very nearly won the race. Another result, however, was that his units became badly strung out; the remainder of Longstreet's corps was coming in with little trouble, but Anderson and Ewell had to stop frequently to fight off Sheridan's slashing attacks from their left, and Gordon was constantly bedeviled by II Corps.

By 11 a.m., Anderson was still five miles from Rice's Station. Ahead of him were the two forks of Sayler's Creek, a tributary of the Appomattox River. He was nearing a crossroads called Holt's Corners when he had to halt and face his brigades west to fend off another onslaught by Crook's horsemen. Someone had decided to let a number of the wagons pass both Anderson and Ewell, apparently to shorten the distance between Ewell and Gordon; while this was being done, the gap between Longstreet's rear guard

Deeds of Valor Rewarded

During the one-sided fighting at Sayler's Creek on April 6, Federal soldiers seized 50 Confederate flags, earning for each captor a Medal of Honor, the Union's highest decoration for valor. Two soldiers demonstrated particular fortitude that day in depriving the enemy of their treasured colors.

Private Charles A. Taggart (*right*) of the 37th Massachusetts surprised a squad of Confederates. He fired into their midst, grabbed their banner and raced toward the Union lines. Taggart's comrades thought he was leading an enemy charge and shot at him, but he was only slightly wounded.

When Second Lieutenant Thomas W. Custer (*far right*) of the 6th Michigan Cavalry confronted a Confederate color-bearer, he was shot in the face. But Custer righted himself in the saddle, returned the fire and wrested the flag from the falling man. Jubilant at capturing his second flag in five days, Custer called out to his older brother, General George Custer, "The rebels have shot me, but I've got their flag." Thomas Custer recovered and became the only Federal soldier to receive two Medals of Honor for his deeds.

PRIVATE CHARLES A. TAGGART
37th Massachusetts

LIEUTENANT THOMAS W. CUSTER
6th Michigan Cavalry

and Anderson's van widened even more.

In their befogged condition, neither Anderson nor Ewell thought to tell Longstreet or Lee what was happening to them. Anderson soon had reason to wish he had, for when the wagons moved unprotected into the widening gap, Federal riders led by Custer attacked, killing drivers, cutting horses loose and setting wagons on fire. To protect the rest of the wagons, Ewell ordered those still behind him to take another road, which forked off to the north. Using it, the wagons could cross Sayler's Creek at the confluence of its two branches and make their way westward at a safer distance from the enemy cavalrymen.

General Gordon was not informed of the change, however; when he arrived at the fork in the road, he followed the wagons—as he had been doing all day—off to the north. Thus, Lee's outnumbered army had been split into three diverging parts. Of these, the one made up of Ewell's and Anderson's commands was facing the most immediate danger.

Anderson's brigades crossed Little Sayler's Creek and pushed three quarters of a mile down the road, only to find Federal cavalry in strength blocking their way. All three of Sheridan's divisions were firmly planted across the road and threatening the Confederate left. When Gordon moved off to the north, Ewell no longer had a rear guard. The Federal II Corps continued to chase Gordon, but Sheridan had sent for Wright's VI Corps, which had been put at his disposal by Grant that morning after Meade's abortive advance on Amelia. Wright had been following Sheridan, and now he made a swing to the north from Pride's Church to gain the Rice's Station road and come in behind Ewell. While the infantry came up, Sheridan's horsemen continued their attacks to hold the Confederates in place.

Lieutenant Colonel Frederic C. Newhall of Sheridan's staff described one of the attacks by Colonel Peter Stagg's brigade. "Stagg's men moved out gallantly for a mounted charge, and, as seen from the knoll where General Sheridan was, there never was a prettier panorama of war in miniature than when this brave brigade trotted across the valley and began to go up the slope on which the enemy's infantry was now entrenched. A heavy fire met them, but they pressed on boldly, as if they had an army at their back, and the piff! paff! of their carbines echoed the sputtering fire from the enemy's hillside."

From the valley of Little Sayler's Creek, Private W. L. Timberlake of Georgia saw the Federal VI Corps deploy. "In full view on the valley's eastern brink," he wrote, "the corps was massing into the fields at a double quick, the battle lines blooming with colors, growing longer and deeper at every moment, the batteries at a gallop coming into action front. We knew what it all meant. The sun was more than halfway down, the oak and pine woods behind them crowning the hill and laying evening's peaceful shadows on Ewell's line and on Sheridan's; its long afternoon beams glinted warmly and sparkled on the steel barrels of the shouldered arms of moving infantry."

The Georgia private was watching Brigadier General Truman Seymour's division take position, and its troops made up only half of the 10,000 about to move against the Confederates. Shortly, Brigadier General Frank Wheaton deployed two brigades on Seymour's left. With Anderson pinned down by Sheridan's cavalry a mile farther south, Ewell's 3,000 men would be forced to face the infantry on their own. Grimly, Ewell

Major General Andrew A. Humphreys, commander of the Army of the Potomac's II Corps, was a mild, courteous man — except when his orders were poorly executed. Then, said one of his officers, "the General had recourse to flaming outbreaks in which all the vigor of the English language burst forth like a bomb."

formed a line blocking the road, halfway down the hillside, with Custis Lee's Richmond troops on the left, Commodore Tucker's sailors in reserve and his one veteran division, Major General Joseph B. Kershaw's, on the right. The Confederates began to throw up fieldworks to face the coming attack. On a hill across the valley, Major Andrew Cowan, VI Corps's artillery commander, deployed his five batteries around the Hillsman house.

It was about 5 p.m. For a brief time the Federals waited — and, in the silence that preceded the assault, the Confederates gave in to exhaustion. It was an eerie moment. "The little stream bawled peacefully at our feet," recalled Colonel Peter A. S. McGlashan of the 50th Georgia. "The tender flowers of spring were showing above the grass. The hum of insects and the strange silence all around seemed to cast a drowsy spell over the men, and I could see them gradually sinking to the ground and, pillowing their heads in their arms, fitfully dreaming."

The respite was ended by the roar of Federal cannon. For half an hour the Confederates were subjected to what Ewell described as "a terrible fire" from 20 guns blasting case shot at a range of 800 yards. The Southern soldiers could only flatten down and endure the bombardment; there

A defiant artillerist from the Richmond Howitzers, fighting as infantry because his battery's guns were lost, rams home a final shot before retreating from Sayler's Creek. "Those that effected their escape did so under a most terrific fire," a survivor recalled. "Many fell, and from necessity, were left behind to the mercy of the victorious enemy."

was no Confederate artillery to fire back.

Ewell and Anderson discussed irresolutely whether they should try to escape to the west or break through the enemy cavalry. Before they could reach a decision, the Federal infantry advanced.

Sheridan was on hand to direct the infantry assault. Lieutenant Colonel Archibald Hopkins watched him instructing General

Wright: "I saw him make a gesture with his palm turned to the front that said unmistakably that whatever opposed us on the hill opposite was to be pushed out of the way."

Wright's infantry had a difficult approach, however. The Confederate column had been able to use a bridge to get across the creek; the Federals, advancing in line of battle across the adjoining field, had to wade through water up to the waist. Corporal B. F. Jones of the 49th Pennsylvania recalled, "At the foot of the hill we came to a quicksand swamp. As soon as I put my foot on it I knew what it was. I immediately stepped out in front and, jumping from one bunch of grass to another, I reached the other side dry shod, while many of the company got in the mire so deep that they could not get out without assistance." There was a sputtering of musketry as Ewell's skirmishers fell back, and then another uncanny silence. The attackers had been told to hold their fire until they were within 200 yards of the enemy line; Ewell's men were ordered not to fire until commanded to do so. As the opposing ranks closed, some of the Federals of Colonel Oliver Edwards' brigade fluttered handkerchiefs at Ewell's men, inviting the Confederates to surrender. The answer was a roar of musketry.

Major Robert Stiles — commanding a detachment in Colonel Stapleton Crutchfield's former Heavy Artillery brigade — called out to his men: Ready! They rose to one knee in unison, he remembered proudly, "like a piece of mechanism." When he shouted Aim! the advancing bluecoats had come so close that he was sure they could hear him distinctly. The Confederates leveled their muskets. Fire!

At the eruption of flame and smoke, Stiles

A Confederate officer urges his embattled men to save their colors after the collapse of Kershaw's line at Sayler's Creek. The engraving was made from Gilbert Gaul's dramatic painting *With Fate against Them*.

said, the first rank of Federal soldiers in front of his position simply disappeared. A moment later, as another volley rang out, the 2nd Rhode Island and the 49th Pennsylvania, in the center of the assault line, broke and ran. Stiles's cannoneers and Major William S. Basinger's 18th Georgia Battalion charged wildly after them, driving the hapless Federals back across the creek with a ferocious combination of bayonet work and point-blank rifle fire.

A Confederate sharpshooter noted that they "clubbed their muskets and used the bayonet savagely." In the fighting, Stiles found himself in possession of his battalion's flag; five soldiers had already fallen while carrying it. The major prudently stuck it upright in some thick brush as a rallying point for his command.

By this time, Edwards' remaining regi-

ments had recovered from the shock of the Confederate counterattack. They wheeled right and opened a devastating fire. The 37th Massachusetts used their Spencer repeaters, and the Federal artillery on the heights hurled canister into the Confederates now exposed on the hillside. Stiles and Basinger led their men through a protective ravine back to the hilltop.

Stiles now found himself without a commanding officer. Crutchfield had ridden off, under heavy fire, to get instructions from Custis Lee; but Crutchfield never reached him. His body was found on the field, shot through the head.

Although their center had been driven in, the Federals continued a grinding assault on both flanks. Colonel William S. Truex brought his brigade up the hill and wheeled left, striking part of Custis Lee's flank and

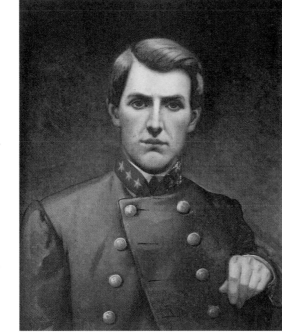

Colonel Stapleton Crutchfield, commanding the Heavy Artillery brigade in Custis Lee's division, suffered a mortal wound during the heaviest fighting at Sayler's Creek. The 29-year-old Virginian, who had served as Stonewall Jackson's chief of artillery until he lost a leg at Chancellorsville, was among the many disabled Confederate officers recalled to action during the War's desperate last months.

sending it back in confusion. On the far right, part of Colonel Joseph E. Hamblin's brigade pushed across the Confederates' rear. Brigadier General James P. Simms's Georgians, holding Kershaw's right flank, were almost surrounded before they ran to escape the trap.

The Confederates' situation was hopeless. They were badly outnumbered, inexperienced and weary; their commanders were too tired to think straight. In a moment, said Stiles, "we were attacked simultaneously front and rear, by overwhelming numbers, and quicker than I can tell it the battle degenerated into a butchery and a confused melée of brutal personal conflicts. I saw numbers of men kill each other with bayonets and the butts of muskets and even bite each other's throats and ears and noses, rolling on the ground like wild beasts."

Private Samuel Eddy of the 37th Massachusetts was pinned to the ground by a bayonet thrust through his body. Yet he managed to chamber another round in his Spencer repeater and kill his assailant. Then, recalled a comrade, Eddy "threw aside the body with one hand as though it were the carcass of a dog, withdrew the bayonet from his own horrible wound, rose to his feet and walked to the rear." Eddy was fortunate. During the fight, Confederate Captain McHenry Howard recalled, "there were no facilities for taking off the wounded, so they were directed, when able, to crawl behind trees and into gullies. It is probable that many were shot a second time, while so lying on the exposed hillside."

While Wright, urged on by Sheridan, launched the infantry assault on Ewell, the Federal cavalry under Wesley Merritt had attacked Anderson's command from the opposite direction. That fight was as fierce as Ewell's, and the outcome was similarly preordained. Anderson had the remnants of two divisions, about 6,000 men under Bushrod Johnson and George Pickett, which he gamely deployed in the face of Merritt's three divisions of horsemen, 8,000 strong.

Crook, leading the largest of the Federal divisions, slammed into Johnson's line. Matthew Ransom's North Carolinians, holding Johnson's left, were flanked out of their shallow trenches and overrun by Colonel J. Irvin Gregg's 1,300 veteran Pennsylvania cavalrymen. The Confederates waited "until the horsemen were almost near enough to leap over the slight breastwork," recalled Major Henry E. Tremain, of Crook's staff. "The quiet line of dingy greys suddenly sprang to life, planted their rebel flags almost within reach of the bold troopers, and with their peculiar faint cheer delivered into them a most destructive volley. Many saddles were emptied but on they came, jumping over the works and killing many with the hoofs of the horses."

Pickett managed to fight off several attacks by Custer's men, supported by Thomas Devin's division, but it was to no avail. Custer finally smashed through with a char-

Troops of Lieutenant General Richard S. Ewell's corps raise their muskets in surrender on April 6, 1865, after the Battle of Sayler's Creek. Among the 2,000 men captured were Ewell himself and five other generals, including Major General George Washington Custis Lee (*left*), eldest son of Robert E. Lee.

acteristically headlong mounted charge, a feat rarely tried against breastworks.

The Confederates "lost all formation and went across the country," said Noble D. Preston of the 10th New York Cavalry, "our boys chasing up and gathering them in." The Federals captured the Confederate wagon train, setting it ablaze after appropriating anything that caught their fancy. Some of Anderson's men, fleeing northeastward, got mixed up with Ewell's men, who were racing to the southwest. Others tried to form a hollow square, the traditional defense against cavalry, but they were soon overwhelmed and forced to surrender. General Henry A. Wise halted his retreating brigade long

enough to stop the Federal pursuit momentarily; then, joined by William Wallace's brigade, he hurried toward Farmville. Anderson and his division commanders managed to get away, but Ewell and seven other generals were taken prisoner, along with about 6,000 men.

At dusk, after most of the Confederates had given themselves up, General J. Warren Keifer, riding alone, found himself facing the leveled muskets of the Naval Brigade, whose men had withdrawn to the woods and were unaware of the surrender. His life was spared when a Confederate officer knocked aside the musket barrel of a man who was about to fire. Keifer rode at top speed back

Colonel Arthur Herbert of the 17th Virginia took command of Brigadier General Montgomery D. Corse's brigade after Corse was captured at Sayler's Creek. By then, the brigade had been worn down to fewer than 300 men; when Herbert enlisted in 1861, his regiment alone had numbered more than 600.

to his own command and returned with them to demand and receive Commodore Tucker's surrender.

About the time VI Corps began the bombardment of Ewell's forces, Gordon had found himself in similarly desperate straits. The road he was following ran northwest for two miles, then turned to the left, descending into a swampy valley and crossing the two forks of Sayler's Creek just above their confluence. The crossings presented a serious bottleneck to the passage of the wagons, and at 4 p.m., one of the two bridges collapsed, slowing Gordon's column just as the relentless Humphreys advanced on its rear.

Gordon formed a line of battle on the crest of the ridge east of Sayler's Creek and prepared to fight. He dispatched a message of quiet alarm to Lee: "So far I have been able to protect the wagons, but without assistance can scarcely hope to do so much longer." The divisions of Nelson Miles and Francis Barlow attacked, driving General Gordon's line from the ridge. The Confederates had managed to position some guns across the creek, and their fire momentarily stopped the Federal attack at the crest. But, as Private Carlton McCarthy recalled, when a shell killed a Federal color-bearer, "the battle line broke into disorder and came swarming down the hill, firing and yelling." Although the Confederates fought savagely, they were forced back among their wagons and against the creek.

"General Gordon, seeing resistance was hopeless," wrote Private Henry T. Bahnson, "gave us orders to save ourselves, showing us the way by galloping his horse down the hill and fording the creek." On the opposite ridge Gordon pulled together what remained of his force and marched to the southwest, toward the High Bridge and Farmville. But he had to leave behind 1,700 men who were taken prisoner, 200 wagons, 70 ambulances, three guns and 13 battle flags.

Even after Lee and Longstreet figured out what was happening to their unexpectedly fragmented army, they were unable to send help to either Gordon or Ewell. Ord was advancing from the southeast, threatening the Confederates' railroad life line; with Sheridan and VI Corps to the east and II Corps to the northeast, Longstreet did not dare weaken his grip on the roads leading to Farmville. The army's only chance was to get to Farmville, cross the bridges and burn them; with the Federals blocked by the flooded river, the Confederates might get some food and rest. The best Longstreet could do was post Mahone's division along the bluffs that lined the west bank of Big Sayler's Creek and await developments.

As evening came on, Lee rode with Mahone, who had returned from sick leave, to look down into the Sayler's Creek valley. It was a scene, Mahone wrote, that "beggars description — hurrying teamsters with their teams and dangling traces (no wagons), retreating infantry without guns, many without hats, a harmless mob, with the massive columns of the enemy moving orderly on.

"At this spectacle General Lee straightened himself in his saddle, and, looking more the soldier than ever, exclaimed, as if talking to himself, 'My God! Has the army dissolved?' "

Deeply moved, Mahone took a moment to steady his voice. He then responded, "No, General, here are troops ready to do their duty."

Recovering his aplomb, Lee ordered Mahone to form a line and rally the stragglers; then he sat his horse and watched, clutching a battle flag.

Never before had the Army of Northern Virginia sustained such a defeat as it had that day. The 8,000 casualties it had suffered since morning amounted to roughly one fourth of its total strength. Needing to get south and join Johnston, the army instead had been deflected to the northwest, away from its route toward Burkeville and Rice's Station.

The only good news Lee received that evening was that bacon and cornmeal to feed his army had definitely arrived in Farmville. On that slender reed he again set to work, gathering scattered commands, assigning routes,

urging his officers and men forward on yet another all-night march. There were only two corps now. Gordon's, which included the survivors of Anderson's corps and Pickett's division under the command of General Wise, was to make its way over the Appomattox at the High Bridge and then west to Farmville. Longstreet's was to take the road northwest from Rice's Station to Farmville — with Mahone's division acting as the rear guard.

That night, Sheridan sent an exultant report to Grant detailing the victory at Sayler's Creek and concluding: "If the thing is pressed I think Lee will surrender." Grant relayed Sheridan's message to President Lincoln, who was still at City Point, and received an immediate response: "Let the thing be pressed."

Thus the frantic chase went on, the Confederates staggering through the night and the Federals taking time to eat and sleep before resuming the pursuit. In his camp that evening, Nelson Miles watched as "a scene of comedy was enacted about the bivouac fires. Several of the wagons were found loaded with the assets of the Confederate Treasury. A Monte Carlo was suddenly improvised in the midst of war. Spreading their blankets on the ground by the fires, the veterans proceeded with the comedy, and such preposterous gambling was probably never before witnessed. Ten thousand dollars was the usual ante; often twenty thousand dollars to come in; a raise of fifty thousand to one hundred thousand was not unusual and frequently from one million to two million dollars were in the pool."

At first light on April 7, two of Sheridan's cavalry divisions, followed by V Corps, swung to the left to keep the Confederates

Buglers sound the advance for a battery of Federal artillery going into action against Lee's retreating troops. "All of our horse artillery was splendid," a staff officer wrote, "commanded by young and dashing fellows whose delight was to fight with the cavalry in an open country, where they could run a section up to the skirmish line and second the carbines with their whistling shells."

from turning south. Ord's Army of the James, VI Corps and Crook's cavalry dogged Longstreet, and II Corps continued to pursue Gordon. Lee's plan now was to provision his men from the railroad cars at Farmville and then cross the Appomattox River as soon as possible.

Once on the north side of the Appomattox, the Confederates could burn the bridges and get a little breathing room, since the river was too high to be forded by infantry. After eating and resting they could continue west toward Lynchburg, then see about uniting with Johnston. Longstreet's

artillery chief, Brigadier General E. Porter Alexander, protested in vain that crossing the river would make them take an indirect route and would leave the shorter road to the Federals.

By early morning, Longstreet's men were filing through the streets of Farmville to draw their rations from the waiting boxcars. Food in hand, they crossed to the open fields on the other side of the river to build their fires, fry their bacon and cook their cornbread. As Gordon's units came in from the northeast, they were met with rations brought across the river for them. General

Lee had just begun to look less worried when he got word that Sheridan's cavalry and Ord's two corps were approaching more rapidly than he had expected. The Confederates on the north side of the river were forced to wolf down their uncooked food, or abandon it, and rush into formation to meet the threat. The supply train was quickly pulled out of Farmville while thousands of Longstreet's men who had not yet drawn their rations watched in dismay, then dashed across the river. Some had to cross on bridges that were already burning.

At the same time, a new threat loomed from the east. There had been an unaccountable delay in setting fire to the High Bridge

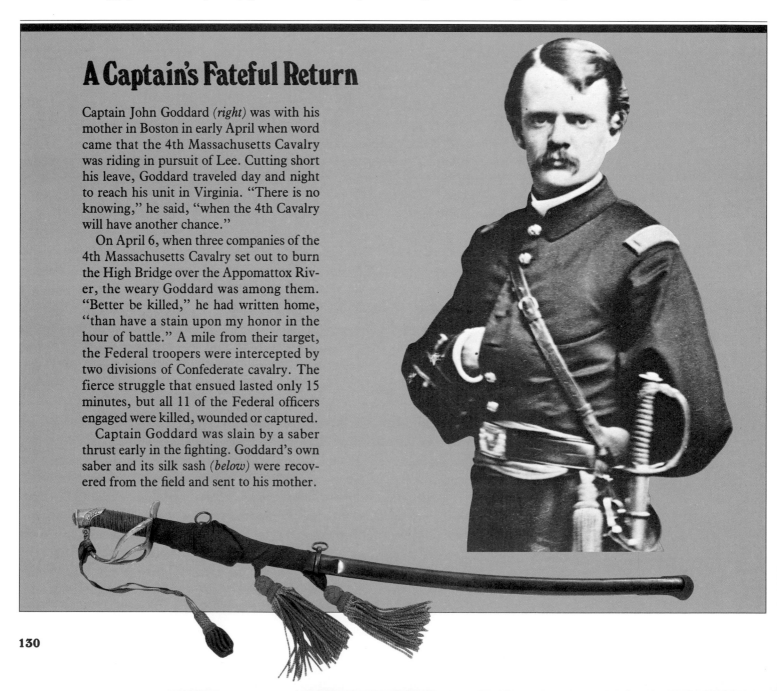

A Captain's Fateful Return

Captain John Goddard (*right*) was with his mother in Boston in early April when word came that the 4th Massachusetts Cavalry was riding in pursuit of Lee. Cutting short his leave, Goddard traveled day and night to reach his unit in Virginia. "There is no knowing," he said, "when the 4th Cavalry will have another chance."

On April 6, when three companies of the 4th Massachusetts Cavalry set out to burn the High Bridge over the Appomattox River, the weary Goddard was among them. "Better be killed," he had written home, "than have a stain upon my honor in the hour of battle." A mile from their target, the Federal troopers were intercepted by two divisions of Confederate cavalry. The fierce struggle that ensued lasted only 15 minutes, but all 11 of the Federal officers engaged were killed, wounded or captured.

Captain Goddard was slain by a saber thrust early in the fighting. Goddard's own saber and its silk sash (*below*) were recovered from the field and sent to his mother.

and its companion wagon bridge. At one point during the night, some of Gordon's men had panicked and stampeded across the wagon bridge in what one participant described as "a mass of wriggling humanity wedged so tightly that moving or even breathing seemed impossible." Several men were trampled, and at least one unfortunate soldier was forced over the side of the bridge. All of Gordon's survivors were across before sunrise, but for some reason, Mahone withheld the order to fire the bridges, and they were not torched until minutes before Humphreys' men arrived at the river.

Sharpshooters tried to keep the Federals at bay, but skirmishers from the 19th Maine were able to extinguish the flames on the wagon bridge with blankets and water from their canteens. Others were able to control the fire on the High Bridge so that only four of its 21 spans were destroyed. After only a brief pause, the Federals continued their pursuit of Gordon and Mahone (who before the year was out would be named president of the railroad company whose bridge he had just inadvertently saved).

While Humphreys led Miles's and Philip de Trobriand's troops northwest to head off Longstreet, a third division, under General Barlow, headed southwest along the railroad track toward Farmville. Barlow's division attacked Gordon's departing wagon train just outside Farmville, cutting off and destroying a number of wagons. But Gordon's rear guard was still fighting hard and exacting a heavy toll: More than 130 of Barlow's men were taken prisoner. Among the Federal casualties was Brigadier General Thomas Smythe, who was mortally wounded. Smythe would be the last Federal general killed in the War.

During the attack, Private Henry Bahnson of the 1st North Carolina Battalion found himself in an awkward predicament. Bahnson approached a railroad cut and discovered that it was "full of Blue Coats, every man with his hands up, and crying, 'Don't shoot, Johnnie! We give up Johnnie!' To say I was surprised wouldn't begin to explain my feelings. If one of them had pointed a gun at me, it would have afforded me infinite pleasure, under the circumstances, to give myself up, but they seemed so anxious to surrender that I leveled my gun at them, and with a variety of emphatic and peremptory expletives, hurried them out before they had a chance to change their minds."

A few more Confederates joined Bahnson, and together they rooted additional Federals out of the cut. One of the prisoners looked around and exclaimed, "Why, is this all of you?" Before they could react, however, the prisoners were hustled to the rear, where a count revealed that there were 103 of them, mostly from the 59th New York and the 7th Michigan regiments.

Crook's horsemen, who by now had entered Farmville from the south, only to find the bridges destroyed, splashed across the river at a ford a mile or so downstream. About 4 that afternoon, they attacked another wagon train. The Confederate cavalry protecting the train countercharged, catching the Federal brigade on a narrow plank road where it was constricted on each side by high fences. They took several more prisoners, including Colonel Gregg, and drove the Union riders toward the river. The Federals rallied, but not before the Confederates had been reinforced by William G. Lewis' North Carolina brigade and 12 guns belonging to the Washington Artillery. In the counterat-

tack General Lewis was wounded and fell into Federal hands, but his men forced the enemy to retreat across the river.

Mahone's rearguard division had entrenched that morning near Cumberland Church, about three miles north of Farmville, where the road taking Lee's army to Lynchburg met the road from the High Bridge along which Humphreys was advancing with his two divisions. The Federals reached the junction early in the afternoon, and by then 18,000 infantrymen of the Army of Northern Virginia were in line, supported by Colonel William T. Poague's battalion of 16 guns. Brief skirmishing convinced Humphreys that he would need help; he sent for Barlow's division and called on Meade to dis-

patch another corps north from Farmville.

Humphreys was not aware that neither VI Corps nor the Army of the James could get across the river at Farmville. When he heard the firing of Crook's engagement in mid-afternoon, he thought reinforcements were on the way and attacked. Nelson Miles's division slammed into Mahone's left and began to turn the Confederate flank. Miles's Federals charged with reckless enthusiasm; General Longstreet observed tartly that they seemed to expect another rout like the one at Sayler's Creek. The Confederates, however, were anything but easy prey. When Colonel George W. Scott's brigade overran Captain Arthur B. Williams' North Carolina battery, taking several of its guns, Mahone reacted

High Bridge, the lofty half-mile-long railroad span over the Appomattox near Farmville, was "a stupendous affair," said a Federal private, on which "a train of cars looks like a toy." The Confederates saved the bridge from a Federal party sent to destroy it on April 6, then burned part of it themselves on their retreat the next day. Pursuing Federals used the wagon bridge at lower right.

quickly. He ordered a body of soldiers from Major General Bryan Grimes's North Carolina division, which had just arrived from Farmville, to counterattack along with some of Anderson's Georgians. They soon recovered the guns.

General Mahone conceded later that the Federal attack had been a very near thing; one enemy brigade had pushed "full around my left flank and were forcing into the rear of my line when General Longstreet cut them off and quite annihilated it." Humphreys had no support — Barlow's division could not get in position to help until dark — so he suspended the fighting until morning, knowing that Lee would slip away during the night. But the Confederates had been delayed another half day at Cumberland Church, while not far to the south Sheridan again was racing westward.

On the night of April 7, General Grant stayed at the Prince Edward Hotel in Farmville, where Lee had stayed the night before. He sat on the hotel porch and watched the Federal VI Corps come into the town. Despite all the marching they had done, remembered Colonel Horace Porter, the soldiers were in high spirits. They "came swinging through the main street of the village with a step that seemed as elastic as on the first day of their toilsome tramp. It was now dark, but they spied the general-in-chief watching them with evident pride from the piazza of the hotel as they marched past.

"Then was witnessed one of the most inspiring scenes of the campaign," continued Porter. "Bonfires were lighted on the sides of the street; the men seized straw and pineknots, and improvised torches; cheers arose

from their throats, already hoarse with shouts of victory; bands played, banners waved, and muskets were swung in the air. A regiment now broke forth with the song of 'John Brown's Body,' and soon a whole division was shouting the swelling chorus of that popular air, which had risen to the dignity of a national anthem. The night march had become a grand review, with Grant as the reviewing officer."

Grant enjoyed the celebration, but he was also deeply thoughtful. He had spoken that day to a Federal surgeon who had been born in Virginia and was related to a captured Confederate general, Richard Ewell. The doctor reported that Ewell was depressed and thought the Confederate cause was lost. They should really have quit sooner, Ewell had said, while they still had a right to claim concessions. If Ewell was feeling that way, Grant decided, Robert E. Lee might be feeling much the same.

That night, Grant received word from Sheridan that Lee's supplies were at Appomattox Station — 26 miles west of Farmville. Sheridan intended to start for the junction the following day; if he could beat Lee to those rations, the chase might be over.

Before Grant went to bed that night, he addressed a short message to his Confederate adversary. "The results of the last week must convince you of the hopelessness of further resistance on the part of the Army of Northern Virginia," Grant wrote. "I feel that it is so, and regard it as my duty to shift from myself the responsibility of any further effusion of blood, by asking of you the surrender of that portion of the Confederate States army known as the Army of Northern Virginia."

Surrender with Honor

"This was our hour of intense humiliation. So long as we carried our guns we felt something of the dignity of soldiers; but when we tramped away leaving these behind, we felt like a lot of hoboes stranded upon an alien shore."

A. C. JONES, 3RD ARKANSAS, C.S.A., AFTER SURRENDERING AT APPOMATTOX COURT HOUSE

5

The Army of Northern Virginia, somehow still responding to the will of its commanding general, pulled its skeletal remains together after dark on April 7 for yet another march —the third in as many nights. The steady disintegration of the army continued. Men who had remained loyal and optimistic as they marched away from their burning capital, who had since fought and marched and fought again, even after the lack of food and rest had left them barely conscious, had reached the limits of human endurance. In man after man, the will to continue flickered out. Many wandered off into the woods and surrendered to the first blue-uniformed soldier they saw; others sank to the roadside and fell asleep; and some kept up only by dropping their rifles, which had become impossibly heavy.

Lee and Longstreet managed to remain clearheaded. They were together when Grant's demand for surrender was brought in at 9:30 that evening. After reading the message, Lee passed it without comment to Longstreet, who glanced at it and responded tersely, "Not yet."

Lee scratched out a brave sentence of reply to Grant, in which weariness and doubt were not entirely concealed. "Though not entertaining the opinion you express of the hopelessness of further resistance on the part of the Army of Northern Virginia, I reciprocate your desire to avoid useless effusion of blood, and therefore, before considering your proposition, ask what terms you

will offer on condition of its surrender."

Then Lee put his army on the road. Supplies from Lynchburg had arrived by rail at Appomattox Station, 25 miles west of Farmville, and were waiting there without adequate protection. First the Confederates would have to disengage from the attacking Federals and get a safe distance away; then, after a few hours of rest, they would stumble onward. Their objective would be Appomattox Court House, a village two miles northeast of the railroad station.

Remarkably, Lee's disengagement went smoothly, and it became possible to hope again. Some of the rations issued at Farmville had been saved and were now eaten, imparting strength and even a certain buoyancy of spirit to many. As the march resumed on the fine spring morning of April 8, the Federal infantry was trailing far behind and Sheridan's cavalry had eased its attacks on the left. The Confederates knew they would be back, but it was a pleasant change nevertheless.

Before long a courier brought Grant's response to Lee's inquiry about possible terms of surrender. There would be only one condition, said Grant, "that the men and officers surrendered shall be disqualified from taking up arms again against the government of the United States until properly exchanged." This was a far more generous offer than Lee had expected from "Unconditional Surrender" Grant.

Lee handed Grant's message to one of

When a cease-fire was imposed at Appomattox Court House on the morning of April 9, 1865, thousands of troops on both sides were left with loaded muskets. The soldiers removed the rounds from their muzzle-loaders with a threaded tool called a ball screw, attached to the tip of the musket's ramrod. Holes left by the ball screws are evident in the Minié balls above, found west of Appomattox along the line of the Federal V Corps.

his aides, Colonel Charles S. Venable. "How would you answer that?" Lee asked.

"I would answer no such letter," Venable declared hotly. "Ah," said the general, "but it must be answered."

By evening, Lee had dispatched his reply and his army had gone into bivouac northeast of Appomattox Court House. General Pendleton, the army's chief of artillery, rode ahead, through the village to the railroad station. An advance detachment commanded by Brigadier General R. Lindsay Walker, consisting of 24 pieces of artillery and two companies of cannoneers who were now serving as infantry, had camped there, near the army's wagon train.

Pendleton was talking with Walker when suddenly the camp was attacked by the vanguard of Custer's cavalry. The startled artillerists grabbed their muskets, got a few of their cannon into action and beat off their assailants. Pendleton, thoroughly alarmed by the presence of the enemy in front of the army, went back to headquarters to report the danger. On the way he narrowly escaped capture by more Federal horsemen, who were cantering along the road between him and the town.

Pendleton had intended to ask that infantry be sent to protect Walker's guns, but at 9 p.m. he heard a brief roar of artillery from the southwest, which was followed by a profound silence. Pendleton guessed its meaning, and when he arrived at Lee's headquarters, he reported that Walker's camp had been overrun.

Although the Confederate high command would not know it for certain until the next day, Pendleton was right. Sheridan's riders had eased up on the Confederate army's left that day in order to devote all their energy to getting in front of it. That afternoon Custer's division had taken Appomattox Station, with its four freight trains loaded with precious food. While the rest of the cavalry was coming up, Custer had gone on to capture the wagons and guns parked nearby. That evening a handful of troopers from the 15th New York Cavalry, led by Lieutenant Colonel Augustus I. Root, charged into the streets of Appomattox itself before being forced to retreat by superior numbers of Confederates. Colonel Root was shot dead from his horse when he was within 15 paces of the courthouse.

As the night deepened, Lee and his generals could see the painful evidence of their predicament. Although Lee's pursuers—II and VI Corps—were still 10 miles to the east, the red glow of enemy campfires burnished the sky to the south, where General Ord's three divisions, after marching along a parallel road, had drawn even with the Confederates. To the west was Sheridan's cavalry, "hovering around," one Virginian recalled, "like ill-omened birds of prey, awaiting their opportunity."

Lee summoned his top commanders to a council at his spartan camp—the headquarters baggage had been lost, and he had no tent, no table, not even a stool. Quietly, he reviewed the situation. A Federal force of some kind undoubtedly was ahead, between them and Lynchburg. Perhaps it was time to give up. Lee's dignity in this extremity reinforced John Gordon's admiration. "We knew by our own aching hearts that his was breaking," Gordon wrote. "Yet he commanded himself, and stood calmly facing and discussing the long-dreaded inevitable."

Confederate artillerymen from General R. Lindsay Walker's brigade dismantle a cannon on the night of April 8, to prevent it from falling intact into the hands of Custer's cavalry. Behind them, other soldiers destroy the railroad track leading west from Appomattox to Lynchburg.

Somehow the generals found the strength to say, as Longstreet had the previous night, "Not yet." If their route was blocked by cavalry alone, without the support of infantry, they still might be able to break through toward Lynchburg.

Gordon, it was decided, would attack westward at first light, with the support of Fitzhugh Lee's cavalry. If Gordon could drive off the Federals in front of them, he would wheel to the south and guard the road while the remaining supply wagons and Longstreet's corps passed through. No one said it, but if Gordon ran into Federal infantry, the cause was lost. Lee admitted as much after the meeting, when he indulged in a moment of black humor. Gordon sent a staff officer back to Lee with a question: After the breakthrough, where was he supposed to stop for the night? Lee stared at the officer. "Tell General Gordon that I should be glad for him to halt just beyond the Tennessee line." Tennessee was 200 miles away.

The stress was beginning to tell on General Grant. All day on April 8 he rode behind II Corps, staying as close as possible to Lee in order to expedite communications between them. Around midday Grant was beginning to suffer from what General Meade's aide, Theodore Lyman, described as "one of his sick headaches, which are rare but cause him fearful pain, such as almost overcome his iron stoicism."

Grant's distress intensified, and when he stopped for the night at a farmhouse near Curdsville, he sought relief by bathing his feet and applying mustard plasters to his

wrists and to the back of his neck. He and his staff had outdistanced their wagons, and so they were forced to appropriate food and blankets from Meade's staff, who shared their billet. Then Grant lay down and tried to sleep. He was still awake at midnight when a courier brought Lee's response to his surrender terms.

The message was a stunning disappointment; Lee, apparently braced by a day of relatively good fortune, had changed his tone completely. "I did not intend to propose the surrender of the Army of Northern Virginia," he wrote. "To be frank I do not think the emergency has arisen to call for the surrender of this army." Lee asked to meet Grant between their lines the next day at 10 in the morning—not to negotiate a surrender, but merely to see how, as Lee put it, "your proposal may affect the Confederate States forces under my command and tend to the restoration of peace."

The ending of the War, in contrast to the surrender of Lee's army, was a task that President Lincoln had reserved for himself and had ordered Grant to avoid. What was more, it seemed to Grant as well as his staff that Lee had taken a more exalted stance than his position merited. One of the staff officers wrote later that the note was "disingenuous," and must have been prompted by "a sudden, vagrant hope of last-minute deliverance."

Grant shook his throbbing head in great dismay. "It looks as if Lee still means to fight," he said. Grant lay down again to wrestle with his pain and try to sleep. But there was a piano in the house, and some of the staff officers pounded on it for hours that night, adding thoughtlessly to the agony of their commanding general—who

hated music even when he was not in pain.

On the far side of the Confederate army, in a cottage near Appomattox Station, General Sheridan was also unable to sleep. An officer saw him at a late hour "stretched at full length on a bench before a bright open fire, wide awake, and evidently in deep thought." All night long Sheridan fretted, consulted with his division commanders and sent messengers riding through the dark.

Sheridan had Lee's supplies, and he was in front of the Confederate army; but he knew he could not bring Lee to bay without infantry support. At the moment he had none. Sixth Corps had reverted to Meade's control, and the nearest foot soldiers were those of Ord's Army of the James. They were coming as fast as they could—traveling 21 hours in 24, and covering 30 miles in that time—but Sheridan sent repeated messages urging them to push even harder.

At last, Sheridan's nightlong vigil was rewarded: General Ord arrived to report that his army was approaching. Ord outranked Sheridan, but he listened to the cavalry officer's fervid suggestions for deployment. Around 4 a.m., the first of Ord's troops reached Appomattox Station, with Griffin's V Corps not far behind.

By that time Sheridan, ever more sure that this would be the final day of the War, was at the front. Ahead of his main force Sheridan had deployed a brigade commanded by Colonel Charles H. Smith. During the night, Smith's men had thrown up breastworks across the Lynchburg road, half a mile west of Appomattox Court House and one and a half miles northeast of the railroad station. Behind Smith was the rest of Sheridan's cavalry. Ranald Mackenzie's division from the Army of the James was on the left; George Crook's division held the center; and Wesley Merritt had Thomas Devin's division on the right, with Custer in reserve. The men had had only a few hours of sleep, the generals none at all; but they were ready by the time daylight came — and Gordon launched an assault.

The old II Corps of Lee's Army of Northern Virginia — which had marched to Get-

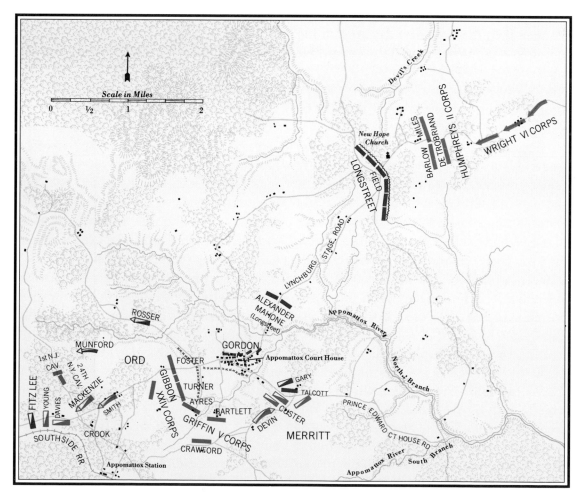

After capturing the Confederate supply trains at Appomattox Station on April 8, Sheridan pushed on toward Appomattox Court House to cut Lee's route to Lynchburg. The next morning, Gordon's corps and Fitzhugh Lee's cavalry successfully attacked Sheridan's positions along the Bent Creek road, but the arrival of Ord's infantry and the envelopment of Gordon's left by Federal cavalry forced the Confederates to fall back on the courthouse. Three miles to the northeast, at New Hope Church, Lee's rear guard under Longstreet turned to engage the Federal II and VI Corps. The opposing forces held these positions until the cease-fire went into effect shortly before noon.

tysburg behind Richard Ewell, to the outskirts of Washington under Jubal Early and to Petersburg with John Gordon — showed its unbreakable spirit that morning. Gordon gestured at the mass of Federal troopers and told his ablest division commander, Major General Bryan Grimes, to "drive them off." While Fitzhugh Lee's cavalry worked its way around the Federal flank, Grimes led three divisions forward in a sweeping attack in echelon from the right.

The firing had already started when Sheridan came up, and with Ord's men on their way he saw no point in making a last-ditch stand. He ordered Smith's brigade to fight a delaying action, falling back to Crook's main line, while Merritt's two divisions moved right to make way for the arriving infantry and to prepare a flank attack.

Giving the Rebel yell, the Confederates soon took possession of Smith's breastworks, and the Federals retreated to Crook's position. Crook and Mackenzie then withdrew to the northwest, Devin and Custer to the southwest, letting a gap open between the wings. Into this opening the joyful Confederates surged, to the crest of a low ridge that previously had been held by the enemy troopers. Then they saw the Federal infantry.

As the morning fog cleared, Fitzhugh Lee and Gordon watched in dismay as masses of blueclad soldiers — Ord's Army of the James — formed on the hillsides to the west. Gibbon's XXIV Corps was already deployed in line of battle, the men lying on their arms for a few minutes of much-needed rest. Behind them a column of black troops — Brigadier General William Birney's division of XXV Corps — was stumbling into place, reeling with exhaustion (one of its brigades had marched 96 miles in three and a half days without losing a single straggler). On Ord's right was Griffin's V Corps. The impact of the Federal presence was overwhelmingly clear. Fitzhugh Lee immediately disengaged and rode away to the west, seeking to avoid the inevitable. "We started for Lynchburg at least 20 miles distant," wrote Private William L. Wilson of the 12th Virginia Cavalry, "officers and men of different regiments jammed up together, always in a trot, sometimes in a gallop." Gordon's infantry, meanwhile, continued to skirmish with an enemy that was no longer retreating but gathering for a massive attack.

To the east of Lee's army, about 8 in the morning, the Federal II Corps resumed its advance. Part of Longstreet's force facing this threat was visible to Sheridan as his cavalry prepared to charge Gordon's left; Lee's two corps would soon be fighting back to back. One of Ord's soldiers described Lee's plight succinctly: "He couldn't go back, he couldn't go forward, and he couldn't go sideways."

The fighting had been going on for three hours when Colonel Venable found Gordon and asked for an assessment of the situation. The message Venable carried back to General Lee was more pessimistic than any Gordon had ever sent to his chief: "I have fought my corps to a frazzle, and I fear I can do nothing unless I am heavily supported by Longstreet's corps."

Lee knew that Gordon would not exaggerate the gravity of his position, and he knew that Longstreet would soon be as much in need of help as Gordon was. As if to himself, Lee murmured: "Then there is nothing left me but to go and see General Grant, and I had rather die a thousand deaths."

Lee had proposed a 10 a.m. meeting with Grant, and although he had not yet received a reply, he assumed that the meeting would take place. But it was still early and he had to wait. In the meantime, he polled his commanders.

Longstreet recalled that he asked Lee whether the bloody sacrifice of his army could in any way help the cause in other quarters; Lee thought not. Then, said Longstreet, "your situation speaks for itself." General Mahone agreed: "It is your duty to surrender," he said. But E. Porter Alexander, Longstreet's chief of artillery, took the opposite view.

"If we surrender this army," said Alexander, "every other army will have to follow suit. All will go like a row of bricks." It would then be impossible for any of them to negotiate acceptable terms, he argued. Instead, Lee's soldiers should be allowed to slip away into the countryside, perhaps to report to the governors of their states and continue the fight.

Lee's answer was sorrowful but firm. "If I took your advice," he said quietly, "the men would be without rations and under no control of officers. They would be compelled to rob and steal in order to live. They would become mere bands of marauders, and the enemy's cavalry would pursue them and overrun many wide sections they may never have occasion to visit. We would bring on a state of affairs it would take the country years to recover from."

"I had not a single word to say in reply," Alexander conceded. "He had answered my suggestion from a plane so far above it that I was ashamed of having made it."

At 8:30 a.m., Lee mounted Traveller and started east to meet Grant. He was accompanied by two staff officers, Colonels W. H. Taylor and Charles Marshall, and by Sergeant G. W. Tucker, the courier who had witnessed A. P. Hill's death. Lee's appearance between the lines caught the Federals by surprise. He had not asked for a truce, and as his party rode past the Confederate pickets, it was met not by General Grant but by an advancing line of II Corps skirmishers. General Humphreys was about to attack

Before the cease-fire was implemented, Confederate artillery fire caused a few final casualties at Appomattox. Private William Montgomery, 15 years old, of the 155th Pennsylvania *(below)* was mortally wounded; Lieutenant Hiram Clark of the 185th New York was killed *(right)*. "A group of sad-eyed officers gathered around the body," said a witness to Clark's death, "and it seemed, under the circumstances, a particularly hard fate."

Longstreet's line. Just then, Lieutenant Colonel Charles A. Whittier appeared with a message from Grant.

While the Federal skirmishers paused, Lee read with dismay that Grant had no intention of meeting him, "as I have no authority to treat on the subject of peace." Yet Grant wrote that he too was anxious to end the hostilities: "The terms upon which peace can be had are well understood. By the South laying down their arms they will hasten that most desirable event."

Lee had no room left for maneuvering. Shots could still be heard on Gordon's front, and fighting was about to erupt on Long-

street's. Lee's negotiating position had suddenly worsened and all mention of the liberal terms that had been offered in Grant's second note had disappeared from the latest correspondence.

With time rapidly running out, Lee told Colonel Marshall to compose a new message reminding Grant of "your proposal of yesterday with reference to the surrender of this army." Again Lee requested a meeting, and this time he did not evade its true purpose.

Lee wanted to wait between the lines for Grant's answer, but the Federal skirmishers began to advance again. Grant had left the area, to ride to Sheridan's position. Hum-

Custer

Bearing a white towel as a flag of truce, Confederate Captain Robert M. Sims *(right)* approaches General Custer in this sketch by Alfred Waud. When Sims asked for a suspension of hostilities, the belligerent Custer replied, "We will listen to no terms but that of unconditional surrender. We are behind your army now, and it is at our mercy."

phreys and Meade had been told to let nothing interfere with their military operations, and neither general felt he had the authority to suspend the attack.

A Federal courier rode out to warn Lee and his party that they were in danger of being overrun by the assault. Stubbornly, Lee stayed. He sent a new message to Grant, requesting "a suspension of hostilities pending the adjustment of the terms of the surrender of this army." Then, with the advancing Federals barely 100 yards away, Lee reluctantly rode back into Longstreet's lines, ordering his men to hold their fire for as long as they could.

And now, remembering that Gordon was still engaged, Lee sent the Georgian instructions to arrange a truce. Captain Robert M. Sims carried word of the cease-fire to Gordon, then rode into the Federal lines, a white towel tied to the tip of his sword. Sims was unable to locate Grant or Sheridan, but he did encounter Custer, who sent two of his staff officers to Gordon, demanding an unconditional surrender.

Gordon refused. Shortly afterward, there arrived at his headquarters a slender, long-haired Federal officer, who was, Gordon said, "of strikingly picturesque appearance." The newcomer swept before Gordon with a flourish, saluted with his saber and proclaimed dramatically: "I am General Custer, and bear a message to you from General Sheridan. The general desires me to present you his compliments, and to demand the immediate surrender of all the troops under your command!"

Since Lee and Grant already were exchanging messages on the subject of surrender, Custer's demand was a breach of military etiquette. Gordon curtly rejected the demand, and Custer responded that Sheridan was prepared to "annihilate your command in an hour." In that case, said Gordon quietly, the responsibility for breaking the truce would be Sheridan's, and Gordon would have nothing more to say. Custer, undeterred, asked to see General Longstreet, and Gordon had him escorted to the senior corps commander. Gordon did, however, take the precaution of sending at least three more truce flags into Federal lines to ensure that a cease-fire was maintained.

Custer's meeting with Longstreet was the stormiest event of that momentous day. Longstreet was in no mood for theatrics. He stared as the 25-year-old general galloped up, blond curls bouncing; another Confederate noted that Custer was wearing "the largest shoulder straps of a major general I ever saw" in addition to "a gorgeous red scarf and in it a gold pin near two inches in length and breadth." In a sharp, agitated fashion, Custer addressed Lee's senior lieutenant: "In the name of General Sheridan I demand the unconditional surrender of this army!"

Longstreet blew up like a powder charge. Custer "was reminded," Longstreet later wrote, "that I was not the commander of the army, that he was within the lines of the enemy without authority, addressing a superior officer, and in disrespect to General Grant as well as myself." When Custer replied that Longstreet would "be responsible for the bloodshed to follow," Longstreet snapped, "Go ahead and have all the bloodshed you want." Custer withdrew.

Meanwhile, General Meade had finally agreed to declare a one-hour truce while couriers raced after General Grant with Lee's latest request for a meeting. Firing had now stopped all over the field. Wearily, Lee threw himself down under an apple tree — General Alexander spread a blanket over some fence rails for him — and, along with his staff, he waited.

Curious about what the cease-fire portended, a group of opposing generals held an informal conference between the lines, in front of Appomattox Court House. General Gibbon recalled that "prominent officers on both sides, who had not met, except in battle, for four years, mingled together and chatted. All wore an air of anxiety, but all seemed hopeful that there would be no further necessity for bloodshed." A Northern correspondent reported that while Generals Longstreet and Ord — the ranking officers present — talked about how best to maintain the cease-fire, the other generals "fraternized in small throngs, and discussed the affairs of the conference and the contents of various flasks that had been brought out especially for the occasion." After about an hour, the officers parted amicably.

A little after 11 a.m., Grant — still unwell — stopped in a clearing to rest from the long ride around his army. Just then, according to newspaper correspondent Sylvanus Cadwallader, a shouting horseman rode up with a letter from Lee. Grant read it impassively, then told Brigadier General John A. Rawlins, his chief of staff, to read it aloud. Rawlins drew a long breath and read Lee's request for a meeting to discuss "the surrender of this army."

There was silence. Someone called for three cheers, but the response was feeble. Then Grant smiled. He suddenly felt wonderful. "When the officer arrived," he said, "I was still suffering with the sick headache; but the moment I saw the note I was cured."

Grant immediately dictated a crisp reply to Lee, explaining his whereabouts and saying he would "push forward to the front for the purpose of meeting you." Grant entrusted the message to Lieutenant Colonel Orville E. Babcock of his staff.

When Babcock came up to Lee and Longstreet, who were waiting under the apple tree, Lee rose and prepared apprehensively for the next step. "General," Longstreet said quietly, "unless he offers us honorable terms, come back and let us fight it out." Impractical as the suggestion was, Lee seemed fortified by Longstreet's unfailing support.

Lee read Grant's note, then mounted and rode west with Babcock to meet the Union commander. Nearing Appomattox Court House, Lee asked Colonel Charles Marshall of his staff to ride ahead and arrange for a meeting place. Marshall spurred his horse on toward the village. Only a few brave inhabitants were outdoors, Marshall noted, and he asked "the first citizen I met to direct me to a house suitable for the purpose."

By one of history's remarkable coincidences, Marshall had come upon a merchant by the name of Wilmer McLean, who once had owned a farm in northern Virginia, near Manassas Junction. In July of 1861, the first major battle of the War had been fought across McLean's land. His home had been used by General Beauregard as his headquarters and later had served as a Confederate hospital; the Yankees had fired a cannon ball into his kitchen.

McLean was a patriotic Southerner, but by March of 1862 he had had enough of soldiers. He took his family away — and avoided by only a few months having to watch the Second Battle of Bull Run, which was fought in his front yard. After several moves, the McLeans settled down in the sleepy little community of Appomattox Court House. "Here," McLean told his family, "the sound of battle will never reach you." But now the War had found them again.

McLean at first tried to avoid his second rendezvous with history. He led Marshall to a vacant, dilapidated building and suggested that the colonel conduct his meeting there. Only when the officer declared the place unacceptable did McLean suggest his own house, the most prosperous-looking residence in the village.

It was a pleasant, tree-shaded, two-story brick structure with a colonnaded porch. Inside, a parlor to the left of the front door contained several chairs and tables. Marshall pronounced it a "fine place for a meeting." He sent word to Lee, who arrived at 1 p.m. accompanied by Colonel Babcock and Sergeant Tucker. About half an hour later, Grant made his way across the porch and entered, followed by a number of his staff officers and by Generals Ord and Sheridan. Lee rose to his feet and the two commanders shook hands.

They were a study in contrasts. Tall, white-bearded and dignified, Lee had put on his best uniform and was wearing his finest sword. Grant was slight and slouched, brown-haired and red-whiskered; his three-starred shoulder straps were sewn on a mud-spattered sack coat. The Union general's field glasses were slung across his shoulder, but he wore no sword. He had the inelegant look, said Staff Captain Amos Webster, of "a fly on a shoulder of beef."

At Grant's behest, Colonel Babcock beckoned several more Federal officers into the crowded parlor. The group now included

Thomas Nast, best known for his political caricatures, finished the 9-by-12-foot canvas at left 30 years to the day after the surrender at Appomattox. Nast relied on his imagination for the décor of McLean's parlor, but he painted detailed portraits of the participants. Generals Sheridan and Rawlins stand at the front of the group of officers at far left, while Colonel Charles Marshall and one of Grant's aides, Orville Babcock, are behind Lee, at left. Nast's son posed for the figure of Grant, clad in the same uniform that the Union general had worn at Appomattox.

Varied Views of the Surrender

No event in the Civil War inspired more works of art than the historic capitulation of Robert E. Lee to Ulysses S. Grant at Appomattox Court House. Yet the artists were hampered by a dearth of accurate details about the interior of Wilmer McLean's house and what transpired there. No photographer was present, nor were any sketches made during the proceedings. In later years an impossible number of officers claimed that they had been in McLean's 16-by-20-foot parlor at the time the surrender was signed — and even the recollections of the men who were actually there were frequently contradictory.

Within minutes after Lee left the McLean house, Federal officers began a feverish hunt for souvenirs of the occasion. By the time the first artists visited the site, the parlor had been refurnished, further complicating their task. But they persisted; three of the best of their efforts are shown here.

One of the earliest versions of the surrender was painted in 1867 by French-born Louis Guillaume, a prominent Richmond artist. Although he utilized sketches of the McLean parlor, his work contains a number of errors. The size of the room is exaggerated, and the tables and chairs painted by Guillaume were replacements for the original furniture, which had been carried off as souvenirs. But the most obvious error was placing Grant and Lee at the same table; in fact, Grant and Lee sat at separate tables, about five feet apart.

The most accurate version of the surrender was painted by Thomas Lovell during the centennial of the Civil War. The proportions of the room are correct, as is the placement of the participants. General Lee and Colonel Marshall are at far left; the officers behind Grant are, from left, Philip Sheridan, Orville Babcock, Horace Porter, Edward O. C. Ord, Seth Williams, Theodore Bowers, Ely Parker and George Custer. Including Custer was one of the artist's few mistakes; by most accounts, he did not enter the McLean parlor.

Brigadier Generals Rufus Ingalls and Seth Williams, and young Captain Robert Todd Lincoln, the President's son. Those who could find chairs sat down; the others stood against the walls. Generals Merritt and Custer arrived while the negotiations were going on but did not enter the room.

As Grant prepared to discuss the surrender, he was seized by a curious emotion. He had been jubilant after receiving Lee's last note. Now, he said, he was "sad and depressed. I felt like anything rather than rejoicing at the downfall of a foe who had fought so long and so valiantly." Grant was also somewhat embarrassed by his rough attire — "afraid," he confessed, "Lee might think I meant to show him studied discourtesy by so coming."

Perhaps as a result of this uneasiness, Grant found it difficult to come to the point of the meeting. He started to talk about other things, chatting about the war in Mexico and old days in the Army, until Lee brought him back to the main topic. "I suppose, General Grant," he said, "that the object of our present meeting is fully understood. I asked to see you to ascertain upon what terms you would receive the surrender of my army."

The Union commander's reply must have lifted an enormous burden from Lee: Grant

Grieving Confederate soldiers cluster around Robert E. Lee as he returns from his fateful meeting with Grant. "Whole lines of battle rushed up to their beloved old chief," a correspondent reported, "and struggled with each other to wring him once more by the hand. Not an eye that looked on that scene was dry."

repeated his original, generous offer. "That is," he explained, "the officers and men surrendered to be paroled and disqualified from taking up arms again until properly exchanged, and all arms, ammunition and supplies to be delivered up as captured property."

Lee suggested that Grant write out the terms, "so that they may be formally acted upon." Grant called for his order book, lit a cigar and for a few moments puffed energetically; he later acknowledged that he did not really know how to begin. Then he reached for a pencil, wrote for a while, paused and wrote some more. He consulted with his military secretary, Lieutenant Colonel Ely S. Parker, made a few changes, then handed the book to Lee.

Now it was Lee's turn to delay; he was clearly reluctant to come to grips with what must have been the most difficult moment of his life. He fidgeted. He cleared a space on a nearby table, put down Grant's order book, took out his steel-rimmed eyeglasses, wiped the glasses with his handkerchief, crossed one leg over the other, carefully put the glasses on and at last picked up the book again. Silently he read:

"In accordance with the substance of my letter to you of the 8th instant, I propose to receive the surrender of the Army of Northern Virginia on the following terms, to wit:

"Rolls of all the officers and men to be made in duplicate, one copy to be given to an officer designated by me, the other to be retained by such officer or officers as you may designate; the officers to give their individual paroles not to take up arms against the Government of the United States until properly" — here Lee, after checking with Grant, borrowed Horace Porter's pencil and inserted the word "exchanged," which Grant had inadvertently omitted — "and each company or regimental commander to sign a like parole for the men of his command.

"The arms, artillery and public property are to be parked and stacked, and turned over to the officer appointed by me to receive them. This will not embrace the side-arms of the officers, nor their private horses or baggage. This done, officers and men will be allowed to return to their homes, not to be disturbed by United States authority so long as they observe their paroles and the laws in force where they may reside."

The last sentence offered far more than Lee could have expected — far more, in all probability, than Grant was authorized to offer. It removed the taint of treason from Lee's soldiers, placing them permanently out of reach of any vengeful Northerners. Lee looked up after he had read it and said quietly: "This will have a very happy effect on my army."

Still Lee hesitated. Something more was on his mind, but he was obviously having difficulty putting it into words. Finally he said: "There is one thing I would like to mention. The cavalrymen and artillerists own their own horses in our army. Its organization in this respect differs from that of the United States. I would like to understand whether these men will be permitted to retain their horses."

"You will find that the terms as written do not allow this," Grant said slowly. "Only the officers are allowed to take their private property."

"No, I see the terms do not allow it," said Lee. "That is clear." He was evidently loath to ask for the favor, but it obviously was important to him.

The Soldiers sharing rations   Description on Back

Grant quickly spoke. "Well, the subject is quite new to me," he said. "I take it that most of the men in the ranks are small farmers, and as the country has been so raided by the two armies, it is doubtful whether they will be able to put in a crop to carry themselves and their families through the next winter without the aid of the horses they are now riding. I will instruct the officers I shall appoint to receive the paroles to let all the men who claim to own a horse or mule to take their animals home with them to work their little farms."

Lee was appreciative. "This will have the best possible effect on the men," he responded with visible relief. "It will be very gratifying and will do much toward conciliating our people."

Now that the terms were agreed upon, Grant asked Lieutenant Colonel Theodore Bowers to copy the order in ink. Bowers was too nervous to write steadily, so Grant gave the assignment to Ely Parker. Meanwhile, Lee told Colonel Marshall to draft the Con-

federate acceptance. While this was being done, Lee explained to Grant that about a thousand Federals had been captured in recent days; Lee wanted to return them as soon as possible, since he could not feed them. "I have, indeed, nothing for my own men," he said. Grant immediately accepted the return of the prisoners and arranged to issue rations to the defeated Confederates.

The two generals signed the terms of surrender and acceptance about 3 p.m. They rose and shook hands again. When Lee led the way back to the porch, the Federal soldiers in the McLean yard came to attention and saluted. Lee returned the salute and paused on the steps.

The Confederate leader stared at the distant hills where his army lay. "He thrice smote the palm of his left hand slowly with his right fist in an absent sort of way," said Porter. Lee then called out in a choked voice for his horse, and when Sergeant Tucker appeared with the animal, Lee reached up and smoothed its forelock. Then he climbed into

On General Grant's orders, Federal soldiers share the rations in their haversacks with famished troops from Lee's army. "The Johnnies had the privilege of strolling into our camps," one Federal recalled, "and were received as though they had been old-time comrades."

150

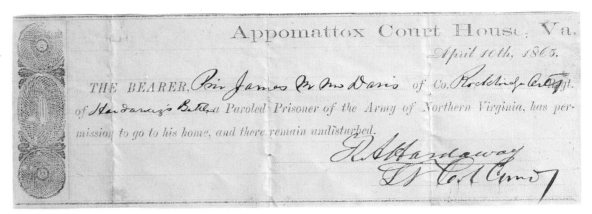

the saddle with an audible sigh — "almost a groan," said Sheridan's aide, Major George A. Forsyth.

Just then Grant, coming down the porch steps, stopped and, without a word, removed his hat. The rest of the Federal officers did the same. Lee raised his hat in return and rode slowly off.

As he came to his own lines, Lee was quickly surrounded by a crowd of soldiers. "Are we surrendered?" someone cried out. It was a moment of overpowering grief; Lee's iron control slipped, and for a time he could say nothing. At last, his voice trembling, his cheeks wet with tears, he spoke to the waiting troops: "Men, we have fought through the war together," he said. "I have done the best I could for you. My heart is too full to say more."

Lee rode away to his headquarters in the apple orchard, where, Confederate Colonel William W. Blackford noted, "he paced backwards and forwards all day long looking like a caged lion." A parade of visiting Union officers — old friends and the merely inquisitive — sought him out. When the visitors were escorted into Lee's presence, Blackford observed, "He would halt in his pacing, and stand at attention and glare at them with a look which few men but he could assume." The visitors would doff their hats respectfully, and soon leave.

Meanwhile, the Federal camps were erupting with joy. As soon as the surrender papers had been signed, crusty George Meade, who had been so sick with stomach troubles and fever for the past week that he had scarcely left his ambulance, mounted a horse and took off down the road at a gallop. Waving his hat and shouting at the top of his voice, he cried, "It's all over, boys! Lee's surrendered! It's all over!"

"The scene in our brigade after General Meade passed was absolutely indescribable," recalled Lieutenant Colonel Charles Weygant of the 124th New York. "Men shouted until they could shout no longer; the air above us was for half an hour filled with caps, coats, blankets and knapsacks, and when at length the excitement subsided, the men threw themselves on the ground completely exhausted." Another soldier told of "huge, lumbering, bearded men" who "embrace and kiss like schoolgirls, then dance and sing and shout, stand on their heads and play at leapfrog with each other."

Throughout the Union army, artillerymen began to fire salutes. "I at once sent word,

During the surrender ceremony on April 12, Confederate forces led by Major General John B. Gordon (*inset, left*) stack their muskets for the last time before the Federal troops of Brevet Major General Joshua Chamberlain (*inset, right*). "The scene was pathetic in the extreme," wrote a Federal soldier, "and tears welled up in the eyes of many a seasoned veteran in the Union lines."

however, to have it stopped," said Grant. "The Confederates were now our prisoners and we did not want to exult in their downfall." To the officers on his staff, Grant said: "The war is over. The Rebels are our countrymen again."

In a moving confirmation of Grant's words, the Federal soldiers parceled out rations to the famished Confederates. A Pennsylvanian in V Corps reported that his regiment "shared their provender with their foemen until every haversack was empty." To the hungry Southern troops the humble fare seemed a feast. "The sweet aroma of real coffee staggered the Confederates," the Pennsylvanian said; "condensed milk and

sugar appalled them, and they stood aghast at just a little butter." With the fraternization came a relaxation of discipline. "There was nothing that resembled guard duty that night," wrote Private Charles Dunn of the 20th Maine. "It resembled a picnic rather than a picket line."

On the morning of April 10, Grant tried to enlist Lee's help in obtaining the surrender of other Confederate armies. Lee declined, because he could not consult with President Davis. With that, Grant's work in Virginia was finished. At noon he and his staff mounted their horses and rode on to Burkeville, where they boarded the train that would carry them to City Point. From there Grant planned to head by steamer for Washington.

Lee did not yet consider himself free to go. For one thing, he felt he could not leave until his soldiers had endured the ordeal of the formal surrender (although he did not intend to watch it). Nor could he go without bidding his troops an official farewell. His last address to his men — General Order No. 9 — was decorous and moving:

"After four years of arduous service, marked by unsurpassed courage and fortitude, the Army of Northern Virginia has been compelled to yield to overwhelming numbers and resources.

"I need not tell the brave survivors of so many hard fought battles, who have remained steadfast to the last, that I have consented to this result from no distrust of them.

"But feeling that valor and devotion could accomplish nothing that could compensate for the loss that must have attended the continuance of the contest, I determined to avoid the useless sacrifice of those whose past services have endeared them to their countrymen.

"By the terms of the agreement officers and men can return to their homes and remain until exchanged. You will take with you the satisfaction that proceeds from the consciousness of duty faithfully performed, and I earnestly pray that a Merciful God will extend to you His blessing and protection.

"With an increasing admiration of your constancy and devotion to your country, and a grateful remembrance of your kind and generous consideration for myself, I bid you all an affectionate farewell."

Only one thing remained to be done. The Confederates had hoped that there would be no formal laying down of arms — that instead they would be permitted to leave their muskets and colors stacked in their encampments for Federal authorities to gather up. But this was one concession Grant would not make. He wanted an official ceremony, something that none of the participants would ever forget — although he ordered that it be kept simple.

On April 10, a six-man commission met at the McLean house and drew up plans for the occasion. Generals Gibbon, Griffin and Merritt represented the Federal army, Generals Longstreet, Gordon and Pendleton the Confederate forces. It was a cordial meeting, and the vanquished commanders acquiesced to all the Federal demands.

The morning of April 12 dawned cold and gray. Brigadier General Joshua Chamberlain, honored with command of the ceremony, aligned his Federal troops on both sides of the road leading through Appomattox; then he watched intently as the Confederate columns crossed the valley and marched up the avenue. There were no bands, no drums, just the familiar shuffling sound of tramping feet, the sun glinting off muskets carried at a right shoulder shift.

"On they come," wrote Chamberlain, "with the old swinging route step and swaying battle flags." General John Gordon led the column; behind him, the first unit in the line of march, was the Stonewall Brigade, now reduced to scarcely 200 men. All the Confederate units, in fact, had shrunk greatly in size — the crimson battle flags were "crowded so thick, by thinning out of men," said Chamberlain, "that the whole column seemed crowned with red."

Gordon sat erect in his saddle, but his head was down and his expression dark. The men behind him, although they kept their lines well dressed and their formation tight under

Major General John Gibbon (*in front of tree*) stands with his staff and an escort of Medal of Honor recipients on May 1, 1865, before presenting 71 surrendered Confederate flags to the War Department in Washington. It was not until 1905 that these revered symbols of the Lost Cause were returned to various Confederate veterans associations.

the scrutiny of their former adversaries, were equally grim.

As the column neared the double line of Union soldiers, Gordon heard a spoken order, a bugle call and an electrifying sound: the clatter of hundreds of muskets being raised to the shoulder. Gordon's head snapped up. Comprehending in an instant, he wheeled his mount toward Chamberlain, "making with the horse and himself," wrote the Union general, "one uplifted figure." As the animal reared, then dipped its head toward the ground, Gordon raised his sword aloft and brought its tip down to his toe in a sweeping response to the Union tribute. He shouted a command, and the advancing Confederates came from a right shoulder shift to shoulder arms — returning the salute.

It was, said Chamberlain, "honor answering honor," and it was hard to say who was more moved. "Many of the grizzled veterans wept like women," said Major Henry Kyd Douglas, commanding John Pegram's old brigade, "and my own eyes were as blind as my voice was dumb." "On our part," Chamberlain wrote, "not a sound of trumpet more, nor roll of drum; not a cheer, nor word, nor whisper of vain-glorying, nor motion of man standing again at the order, but an awed stillness rather, and breath-holding, as if it were the passing of the dead."

After the exchange of salutes, the surrendering soldiers turned to face Chamberlain, dressed their lines, fixed their bayonets and stacked their muskets. They hung their cartridge boxes on the stacks. Then, Chamberlain wrote, "lastly — and reluctantly, with agony of expression — they fold their flags, battle-worn and torn, blood-stained, heart-holding colors, and lay them down." This was the most painful part of the ordeal; said

one North Carolinian: "We did not even look into each other's faces."

In all, 28,231 Confederates were paroled — far more than the 8,000 fighting men Lee had commanded at the very end of the fighting. Until dark on April 12, stragglers kept drifting in. Some were deserters; others had simply been sleeping or trying to find food. Now they needed written passes in order to be able to travel safely home, and so they reappeared.

That night the soldiers of Lee's army began to leave for the distant parts of the South. Lee departed for Richmond, accompanied by Federal cavalry. He had declined the escort, but the troopers insisted on riding with him for at least part of the way, as an honor guard.

The next day, wrote Chamberlain, "over all the hillsides in the peaceful sunshine, are clouds of men on foot or horse, singly or in groups, making their earnest way as if by the instinct of the ant, each with his own little burden, each for his own little house."

By the evening of April 13, most of them were gone, and the Army of Northern Virginia was no more.

There remained, however, 175,000 Confederate soldiers under arms elsewhere. Roughly half of them were scattered throughout the South in various garrisons; the rest were concentrated in the three Confederate armies still in the field. Of these the largest, best organized and most threatening to the Federals was General Joseph E. Johnston's force in North Carolina.

Word of Lee's surrender began to spread through Johnston's army at Raleigh on April 12, as the Confederates were about to yield the state capital to Sherman's advancing

Federals. Johnston had been notified the previous day, but he was reluctant to share the information with his troops. Then paroled soldiers on their way home from Appomattox began to filter into the Confederate lines. At first their story was not believed — some were accused of deserting and were arrested. But on the 12th, the nearby Federal army heard the news and raised a cheer; the truth could not be denied.

Jefferson Davis was not willing to accept the inevitable. Lee's report of the events at Appomattox reached him at Greensboro, North Carolina — the temporary home of the fragmented Confederate States government, now operating out of the railroad cars in which the President and his staff had fled Richmond. Initially, Davis broke down and wept, but he soon pulled himself together and called a remarkable meeting.

Davis summoned General Johnston, who had been returned to command over Davis'

Recently paroled Confederate soldiers take their ease beneath the equestrian statue of George Washington in Richmond's Capitol Square on April 14, 1865. "Once more the beloved gray was everywhere," wrote a Confederate loyalist, "and once more bright eyes regained a little of their brightness, as they looked upon it."

vain objection, and General Beauregard, now Johnston's second-in-command. "We had supposed," wrote Johnston, "that we were to be questioned concerning the military resources of our department in connection with the question of continuing or terminating the war." Instead, Davis talked at length about his plans to raise new troops and fight new battles. He proposed to make up for the loss of Lee's army by rounding up deserters. Most of the missing Confederates, Davis felt sure, had simply gone home so that they could care for their families, and they would soon be back.

Johnston and Beauregard listened in disbelief. "Neither opinions nor information was asked," Johnston wrote. It was not until the next day that Davis finally asked Johnston for his assessment. His reply, said a witness, was so forceful as to be "almost spiteful."

"My views are, sir," said Johnston, "that our people are tired of war, feel themselves whipped, and will not fight. Our country is overrun, its military reserves greatly diminished, while the enemy's military power and resources were never greater, and may be increased to any extent desired." Moreover, he said, the situation was growing steadily worse. Johnston's men regarded Lee's surrender as the end of the War, and he expected "to retain no man beyond the by-road or cowpath that leads to his house. My small force is melting away like snow before the sun, and I am hopeless of recruiting it."

There was a long pause when Johnston had finished. Davis' eyes were fastened on a small piece of paper, which he kept folding and unfolding. Then he spoke in a low voice. "What do you say, General Beauregard?"

Beauregard, whose relations with Davis over the years had been scarcely better than Johnston's, replied steadily: "I concur in all General Johnston has said."

As the discussion went on, the animosity between Johnston and Davis was barely concealed. At one point Johnston commented bluntly that the only real presidential power left to Davis was the authority to end the War. Yes, said the exasperated Davis, but the Federal forces did not recognize him. In that case, rejoined Johnston, why not let the military commanders deal with each other, as was customary in such situations?

Ultimately a letter to General Sherman was prepared — drafted by Davis, but signed by Johnston — that proposed a meeting to discuss a cease-fire. The message asked Sherman to seek "a temporary suspension of operations" not only on his own front but in all theaters, "the object being to permit the civil authorities to enter into the needful arrangements to terminate the existing war." This proposition went beyond a military surrender into the political arena, but Sherman simply ignored the problem.

Sherman quickly agreed to a meeting and to Johnston's request for a broad suspension of operations. He had all the authority he needed to end hostilities in North Carolina, he said, and he would ask Grant to halt any advance of Virginia-based Federal forces into the area. Sherman suggested further that both he and Johnston limit any movement of their troops before their meeting, which was arranged for April 17.

On that day near Durham Station — on the railroad 26 miles northwest of Raleigh — the two generals' parties approached each other under white flags. Along with various aides and generals, Sherman was accompanied by his cavalry chief, Judson Kilpat-

157

rick, and Johnston by his, Wade Hampton. Both commanding generals rode ahead of their escorts and greeted each other with warmth and respect. They had met only as opposing commanders but "knew enough of each other," Sherman said dryly, "to be well acquainted at once."

As the pair rode toward a small house owned by a farmer named Bennett, they presented the same contrast in appearance that had been so evident at Appomattox: The Southern commander, 13 years Sherman's senior, was dignified and well groomed; Sherman was spartan and unprepossessing.

But Johnston's poise was short-lived. Sherman began their meeting by handing Johnston a telegram he had received from Washington just as he left Raleigh. Dated April 15, it began, "President Lincoln was murdered last night in his private box at Ford's theater." Sherman watched Johnston's reaction to the news closely. "The perspiration came out in large drops on his forehead," Sherman wrote later, "and he did not attempt to conceal his distress. He de-

nounced the act as a disgrace to the age, and hoped I did not charge it to the Confederate government."

When the commanders moved on to the subject of their meeting, there was no disagreement between them. Sherman pointed out that since Lee had surrendered, Johnston could follow suit "with honor and propriety." Johnston agreed and he went further; he was ready to surrender not only his army, but — if Jefferson Davis would concur — all Confederate forces still under arms.

Sherman was excited by the prospect of ending the War — and avoiding the danger of continued guerrilla fighting — with what he called "one single stroke of the pen." He pursued the subject. Davis was being difficult, Johnston admitted, but Secretary of War John C. Breckinridge was at hand. Breckinridge was a realist, and he would help persuade Davis to sign what the generals worked out.

Thus, on the following day, the surrender document was negotiated. At this point Sherman went beyond Johnston: The docu-

Major Generals William Tecumseh Sherman and Joseph E. Johnston held their peace negotiations in the modest log home of James Bennett near Durham Station, North Carolina. After the opening presentations, Sherman postponed discussion while he broke out a bottle of whiskey and passed it among the participants.

Sherman's soldiers torch a cartload of New York newspapers that contain articles condemning the generous peace terms their general had given Johnston's Confederates. "This was the last property that I saw destroyed by the men," one officer said, "and I witnessed the scene with keener satisfaction than I had felt over the destruction of any property since the day we left Atlanta."

ment provided not only for the surrender of all Confederate forces, with the men permitted to keep their weapons, but for the readmission of Confederate states to the Union, with full rights of citizenship and no prosecution.

This of course was also far beyond the limits set by President Lincoln when he had warned Grant to deal only with military affairs; but Sherman had not seen that message. He did realize that the agreement he had just made would require the approval of the Union's new President, Andrew Johnson, and he sent it off to Washington. Johnson referred the document to Grant, and when the victorious general read it on April 21, he knew immediately that he held a bombshell in his hands. And indeed Sherman's pact created havoc when it was presented to an emergency session of the Cabinet that night. The assassination of Lincoln had convulsed the capital with grief, rage and suspicion that the dying Confederacy had been somehow responsible for the act.

Leniency was the last thing on the minds of the nation's leaders. Unanimously and angrily they rejected the terms of Johnston's surrender and vilified Sherman for proposing them. Secretary of War Stanton went so far as to suggest treasonous motives, earning sharp dissension from the customarily deferential Grant.

Nevertheless, Grant was ordered to North Carolina to repudiate the surrender agreement and take over from Sherman. He arrived at Sherman's headquarters at Raleigh on April 24. On Grant's instructions, Sherman notified Johnston that the terms of the surrender had been rejected and that unless he surrendered under the same terms given Lee at Appomattox, hostilities would resume in 48 hours.

Jefferson Davis had been sure all along that the North would never agree to the liberal terms Sherman had proposed. When told of the rejection, Davis was ready with new instructions: Johnston was to order his men to disperse, then reassemble somewhere to the southwest — and fight on.

Johnston's response to these commands was caustic. "We have to save the people, spare the blood of the army and save the high civil functionaries," he said. "Your plan, I think, can do only the last." Later, he sent a curt message renouncing Jefferson Davis and charting his own course: "I have proposed to General Sherman military negotiations in regard to this army."

The next day, April 26, Johnston signed a new surrender document based on the one given Lee at Appomattox. As it turned out, Johnston surrendered far more men than had Lee. In addition to his army, Johnston's department included the troops that had been serving in the Carolinas, Georgia and Florida — totaling more than 89,000 in all. The War in the East was over.

When news of the original agreement between Sherman and Johnston reached Lieutenant General Richard Taylor, commanding the Confederate forces in Alabama, he immediately requested a truce. Taylor, son of the Mexican War hero and former President Zachary Taylor, had for some time believed his cause was lost, but he had continued to do his best to stop a two-pronged Federal drive south from Tennessee.

On April 2, Taylor had barely escaped when Selma, Alabama, fell to a 12,000-man cavalry force under Brigadier General James H. Wilson. Only 10 days later, after a three-week siege, Taylor had been forced to abandon Mobile, a stronghold the Union had never been able to take.

When he heard that Johnston had surrendered, Taylor immediately opened negotiations with the Federal commander in Alabama, Major General Edward R. S. Canby. Even after he learned that the Sherman-Johnston agreement had been rejected by the authorities in Washington, Taylor remained determined to surrender. "It seemed absurd," he wrote, "for the few there present to continue the struggle against a million of men." On the 8th of May, at Citronelle, Alabama, Taylor surrendered his army to General Canby with sincere thanks for the generous Federal terms.

Taylor's capitulation left one Confederate army in the field — that of General Edmund Kirby Smith, who commanded the Trans-Mississippi Department. This vast region embraced all the Confederacy west of the Mississippi River: Missouri, Arkansas, Texas and most of Louisiana; the territories of New Mexico and Arizona; and the Indian

A Last Feat of Arms

As Confederate resistance weakened everywhere in March of 1865, Brigadier General James H. Wilson (*below, right*) launched a massive Federal cavalry raid through Alabama and Georgia (*map*). Armed with repeating carbines and supported by three batteries of artillery, Wilson's 14,000 troopers had unprecedented firepower. But their success would hinge on the 27-year-old Wilson's ability to outmaneuver the legendary Nathan Bedford Forrest, whose 6,000 Confederate horsemen were concentrating between them and Selma, Alabama, the most important military supply center in the area.

Wilson was equal to the challenge. On March 22, the Federals occupied Elyton (what is now the city of Birmingham). Then Wilson detached Brigadier General John T. Croxton's brigade to burn Tuscaloosa and divert a division of Forrest's Confederate cavalry, which was approaching from Mississippi. After routing Forrest near the town of Montevallo, Wilson ordered Brigadier General Edward McCook's division to Centreville to block the approach of another of Forrest's divisions. Wilson's main force defeated Forrest again at Ebenezer Church, and on April 2 — the day that Petersburg fell — the Federals carried Selma. Montgomery, Alabama, and Columbus and Macon, Georgia, fell in rapid succession.

On the 20th of April, word of General Lee's surrender to Grant finally brought an end to the fighting. That Wilson's feat of arms came too late to have an impact on the War did not lessen his pride in the achievement. "My cavalry corps was the best in the world," he exulted. "The plain truth is, they were invincible."

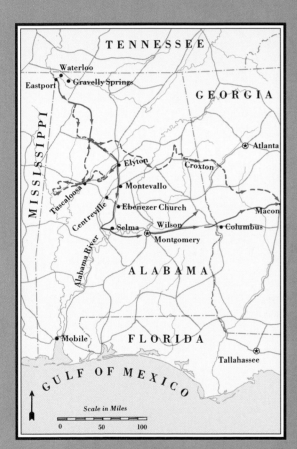

The map above shows the routes that were taken by Wilson's three cavalry divisions (*solid line*) and Croxton's detached brigade (*broken line*) during their 550-mile-long strike from Gravelly Springs, Alabama, to Macon, Georgia. In 29 days, the raiders killed or wounded 1,200 Confederates and captured 6,820 prisoners, 288 artillery pieces and 100,000 stands of small arms; they also destroyed two dozen factories and foundries, seven naval vessels, 600 railroad cars and locomotives, and 235,000 bales of cotton — all at a cost of 715 Federal casualties.

Territory (present-day Oklahoma). In reality, most of this land was in Federal hands.

Kirby Smith's command had been effectively cut off from the rest of the Confederacy since the fall of Vicksburg in 1863. For more than a year he had run the part of the area he controlled as a sort of independent satrapy; it was sometimes referred to as "Kirby Smithdom." Its isolation had been a severe handicap to the South, but after the surrender of Lee and Johnston, its inaccessibility suddenly seemed to offer great advantages. Jefferson Davis, still intransigent, was in fact on his way toward Kirby Smith's dominion with plans to stage a last-ditch fight there.

Davis' stance made it incumbent on Kirby Smith to keep the War going. On April 21, he issued a clarion call to his troops, urging them to "stand by your colors" even though "great disasters have overtaken us." On May 9, he flatly rejected an invitation from Union Major General John Pope in St. Louis to surrender on the same terms granted to Lee and Johnston.

Three days later, two Federal regiments attacked a Confederate outpost called Palmito Ranch, on the Rio Grande. The Federal soldiers captured the place on May 12 but were evicted the same day. They took it once again the following day and were once again driven away, this time for good. At a cost of 115 casualties, the Federal force had just fought — and lost — the last battle of the Civil War.

Meanwhile, Jefferson Davis had been captured on May 11 in Georgia, and Kirby Smith reported that virtually all of the 50,000 soldiers under his command "dissolved all military organization and returned to their homes." Nevertheless, Grant sent

Philip Sheridan to bring peace to the Trans-Mississippi Department.

Sheridan's arrival was enough for Kirby Smith. On May 21, saying that he felt "powerless to do good for my country," he sent his top subordinate, Major General John B. Magruder, to arrange a surrender — not to Pope in St. Louis, but to Canby in New Orleans. Magruder signed the surrender document on May 26, and Kirby Smith signed on June 2.

The South had been shocked by the rapid and anticlimactic conclusion of its long crusade for independence. Instead of "some momentous and splendid crisis of arms," as editor Edward Pollard described it, "the whole fabric of Confederate defense tumbled down at a stroke of arms that did not amount to a battle."

There were, of course, loose ends and ragged edges. The crew of the Confederate cruiser *Shenandoah* continued raiding until August, then sailed for England and surrendered the vessel in Liverpool on November 6. A three-man detachment of Confederate soldiers, sent into Virginia's Dismal Swamp to keep an eye on Federal activities around Norfolk, did not come in from their boggy outpost until July of 1866. They were probably the last Confederates to surrender.

The War had been declared officially over, by presidential decree, in May of 1865, and most people had considered it finished when Lee surrendered on April 9. But for many others, the true conclusion of the bloodiest conflict in America's history came four years to the day after it had begun, with the surrender of Fort Sumter.

On April 14, 1865, four thousand people, most of them from the North, gathered in Charleston, South Carolina, for a special ceremony. They assembled in Fort Sumter and bowed their heads in solemn prayer. Then a sergeant — a member of Sumter's 1861 garrison — stepped forward, and from a leather bag he produced the United States flag that had flown over the besieged fort on the day of its surrender.

The reaction of the crowd was described by a Northern visitor, Mary Cadwalader Jones, who was there with her father. "We all held our breath for a second," she wrote, "and then we gave a queer cry, between a cheer and a yell; nobody started it and nobody led it; I never heard anything like it before or since, but I can hear it now."

Two sailors who had been at the fall of Sumter bent the flag to its halyards, then placed the lines in the hands of the man who had commanded the fort in 1861 — Brigadier General Robert Anderson. The frail and aging Kentuckian, retired for disabilities in 1863, had been a major when he and his men endured the first bombardment and the first Union defeat of the Civil War. Before raising the banner that he had been forced to haul down years ago, General Anderson began to speak.

"At first I could not hear him, for his voice came thickly," Mary Jones recalled. "But in a moment he said clearly, 'I thank God that I have lived to see this day,' and after a few more words he began to hoist the flag.

"It went up slowly and hung limp from the staff, a weather-beaten, frayed and shell-torn old flag, not fit for much more work, but when it had crept clear of the shelter of the walls a sudden breath of wind caught it, and it shook its folds and flew straight out above us."

Barely visible in the throng of cheering spectators, retired Brigadier General Robert Anderson raises the same flag over Fort Sumter on April 14, 1865, that he had pulled down in surrender four years earlier. Calling the ceremony "an act of duty," the ailing, 60-year-old Anderson said simply: "I restore to its proper place this dear flag."

The Vanquished Bastion of Rebellion

For four years, the citadel on the James River had stood as the defiant symbol of Southern independence, frustrating a series of Union generals who exhorted their men to fight "on to Richmond!" And the frustration did not end when U. S. Grant's troops finally marched into

THE STARS AND STRIPES OVER RICHMOND'S CAPITOL AND BURNED-OUT COMMERCIAL BUILDINGS ON THE JAMES RIVER CANAL

Richmond on April 3, 1865. The Confederate government had fled, leaving the heart of the city in flaming ruins.

Still, the fall of the Southern capital foretold the end of the Confederacy. Union soldiers, too war-weary to be vindictive, earned the grudging admiration of Richmond's citizens by controlling the fires and protecting Confederate families and property. Photographers who arrived with the Federal army recorded scenes of devastation and humiliation, as proud but starving civilians lined up to receive handouts of food.

For one matron, the sound of the "Star Spangled Banner," wafting from the capitol (below), evoked bittersweet memories. Before the War, recalled Mrs. Sallie Putnam, the anthem had stirred her patriotism. Now, she wrote, it was "a requiem for buried hopes."

FIRE-BLACKENED DEBRIS IN BANK STREET NEAR THE UNDAMAGED EXCHANGE HOTEL *(BACKGROUND)*

IRON UNDERCARRIAGES IN THE RUBBLE OF THE RICHMOND & PETERSBURG RAILROAD STATION

A WATERWHEEL STILL INTACT IN THE BURNED-OUT PAPER MILL

SKELETAL REMAINS OF RICHMOND'S BUSINESS CENTER, SOON TO BE REBUILT

ACKNOWLEDGMENTS

The editors wish to thank the following individuals and institutions for their valuable assistance in the preparation of this volume:

Montana: Crow Agency — Neil Mangum, Custer Battlefield National Monument.

Pennsylvania: Carlisle Barracks — Randy Hackenburg, Michael J. Winey, U.S. Army Military History Institute. Gettysburg — D. Mark Katz. Harrisburg — Richard A. Sauers.

Pittsburgh — Al Richardson.

Texas: Bryan — John M. Carroll.

Virginia: Alexandria — Frank and Marie-T Wood. Annandale — Homer Babcock. Appomattox — John Montgomery, Ronald G. Wilson, Appomattox Court House National Historical Park. Arlington — John E. Yoho. Fort Belvoir — John M. Dervan, James L. Kochan, U.S. Army Engineer Museum. Richmond — David C. Hahn, Museum of the Confedera-

cy. Waynesboro — Patrick A. Schroeder.

Washington, D.C.: Deborah Edge, Still Pictures Branch, National Archives; Eveline Nave, Photoduplication Service, Library of Congress.

Wisconsin: Milwaukee — Howard Madaus, Milwaukee Public Museum.

The index for this book was prepared by Roy Nanovic.

BIBLIOGRAPHY

Books

Albert, Allen D., ed., *History of the Forty-Fifth Regiment: Pennsylvania Veteran Volunteer Infantry 1861-1865.* Williamsport, Pa.: Grit Publishing Co., 1912.

Alexander, E. P., *Military Memoirs of a Confederate.* Dayton: Morningside Bookshop, 1977 (reprint of 1907 edition).

Barrett, John G.:

The Civil War in North Carolina. Chapel Hill: The University of North Carolina Press, 1963.

Sherman's March through the Carolinas. Chapel Hill: The University of North Carolina Press, 1956.

Barringer, Paul B., *The Natural Bent.* Chapel Hill: The University of North Carolina Press, 1949.

Bearss, Ed, and Chris Calkins, *Battle of Five Forks.* Lynchburg, Va.: H. E. Howard, 1985.

Bosbyshell, Oliver Christian, *The 48th in the War.* Philadelphia: Avil Printing Co., 1895.

Bowen, James L., *History of the Thirty-Seventh Regiment Mass. Volunteers, in the Civil War of 1861-1865.* Holyoke, Mass.: Clark W. Bryan & Co., 1884.

Brewer, A. T., *History: Sixty-First Regiment, Pennsylvania Volunteers: 1861-1865.* Pittsburgh: Art Engraving & Printing Co., 1911.

Bull, Rice C., *Soldiering: The Civil War Diary of Rice C. Bull.* Ed. by K. Jack Bauer. San Rafael, Calif.: Presidio Press, 1977.

Caldwell, J.F.J., *The History of a Brigade of South Carolinians.* Philadelphia: King & Baird, 1866.

Calkins, Christopher M.:

From Petersburg to Appomattox: April 2-9, 1865. Farmville, Va.: The Farmville Herald, 1983.

Thirty-Six Hours before Appomattox: April 6 and 7, 1865. Spotsylvania Court House, Va.: Privately published, 1980.

Catton, Bruce, *Grant Takes Command.* Boston: Little, Brown and Co., 1969.

Chamberlain, Joshua Lawrence, *The Passing of the Armies.* Dayton: Morningside Bookshop, 1981.

Clark, Charles M., *The History of the Thirty-Ninth Regiment Illinois Volunteer Veteran Infantry in the War of the Rebellion.* Chicago: Published by the Regiment, 1889.

Clark, Walter, ed., *Histories of the Several Regiments and Battalions from North Carolina in the Great War 1861-'65.* Vols. 1-4. Wendell, N.C.: Broadfoot's Bookmark, 1982 (reprint of 1901 editions).

Cornish, Dudley T., *The Sable Arm: Negro Troops in the Union Army, 1861-1865.* New York: W. W. Norton & Co., 1966.

Cox, Jacob D.:

The March to the Sea: Franklin and Nashville. Vol. 10 of *Campaigns of the Civil War.* New York: Charles Scribner's Sons, 1882.

Military Reminiscences of the Civil War. Vol. 2. New York: Charles Scribner's Sons, 1900.

Curtis, O. B., *History of the Twenty-Fourth Michigan of the Iron Brigade.* Detroit: Winn & Hammond, 1891.

Davis, William C., *Breckinridge: Statesman, Soldier, Symbol.* Baton Rouge: Louisiana State University Press, 1974.

Douglas, Henry Kyd, *I Rode with Stonewall.* Chapel Hill: The University of North Carolina Press, 1940.

Evans, Clement A., ed., *Confederate Military History.* Vol. 5. New York: Thomas Yoseloff, 1962.

Fisk, Wilbur, *Anti-Rebel: The Civil War Letters of Wilbur Fisk.* Croton-on-Hudson, N.Y.: Emil Rosenblatt, 1983.

Frassanito, William A., *Grant and Lee: The Virginia Campaigns, 1864-1865.* New York: Charles Scribner's Sons, 1983.

Freeman, Douglas Southall:

Gettysburg to Appomattox. Vol. 3 of *Lee's Lieutenants: A Study in Command.* New York: Charles Scribner's Sons, 1944.

R. E. Lee: A Biography. Vols. 3 and 4. New York: Charles Scribner's Sons, 1935.

Gould, Joseph, *The Story of the Forty-Eighth: A Record of the Campaigns of the Forty-Eighth Regiment Pennsylvania Veteran Volunteer Infantry.* Philadelphia: Alfred M. Slocum Co., 1908.

Grant, Ulysses S., *Personal Memoirs of U. S. Grant.* New York: Charles L. Webster & Co., 1894.

Haley, John, *The Rebel Yell & the Yankee Hurrah: The Civil War Journal of a Maine Volunteer.* Ed. by Ruth L. Silliker. Camden, Me.: Down East Books, 1985.

Haskell, John Cheves, *The Haskell Memoirs.* Ed. by Gilbert E. Govan and James W. Livingood. New York: G. P. Putnam's Sons, 1960.

Haynes, E. M., *A History of the Tenth Regiment, Vt. Vols., with Biographical Sketches.* Rutland, Vt.: The Tuttle Co., 1894.

Heth, Henry, *The Memoirs of Henry Heth.* Ed. by James L. Morrison Jr. Westport, Conn.: Greenwood Press, 1974.

Howard, McHenry, *Recollections of a Maryland Confederate Soldier and Staff Officer under Johnston, Jackson and Lee.* Dayton: Morningside Bookshop, 1975 (reprint of 1914 edition).

Howard, Oliver Otis, *Autobiography of Oliver Otis Howard.* Vol. 2. New York: The Baker & Taylor Co., 1907.

Humphreys, Andrew A., *The Virginia Campaign of '64 and '65.* Vol. 12 of *Campaigns of the Civil War.* New York: Charles Scribner's Sons, 1890.

Johnson, Robert Underwood, and Clarence Clough Buel, eds., *Battles and Leaders of the Civil War.* Vol. 4. New York: The Century Co., 1887.

Johnston, Joseph E., *Narrative of Military Operations Directed during the Late War between the States.* New York: D. Appleton and Co., 1874.

Jones, J. B., *A Rebel War Clerk's Diary.* Vol. 2. Ed. by Howard Swiggett. New York: Old Hickory Bookshop, 1935.

LeConte, Emma, *When the World Ended: The Diary of Emma LeConte.* Ed. by Earl Schenck Miers. New York: Oxford University Press, 1957.

Livermore, Thomas L., *Days and Events: 1860-1866.* Boston: Houghton Mifflin Co., 1920.

Longacre, Edward G., *From Union Stars to Top Hat: A Biography of the Extraordinary General James Harrison Wilson.* Harrisburg, Pa.: Stackpole Books, 1972.

Longstreet, James, *From Manassas to Appomattox.* Ed. by James I. Robertson Jr. Millwood, N.Y.: Kraus Reprint, 1981.

Lucas, Marion Brunson, *Sherman and the Burning of Columbia.* College Station: Texas A&M University Press, 1976.

Lyman, Theodore, *Meade's Headquarters 1863-1865: Letters of Colonel Theodore Lyman from the Wilderness to Appomattox.* Ed. by George R. Agassiz. Boston: The Atlantic Monthly Press, 1922.

McCarthy, Carlton, *Detailed Minutiae of Soldier Life in the Army of Northern Virginia 1861-1865.* Richmond: Carlton McCarthy, 1882.

Meade, George, *The Life and Letters of George Gordon Meade.* Vol. 2. New York: Charles Scribner's Sons, 1913.

Miles, Nelson A., *Personal Recollections and Observations of General Nelson A. Miles.* New York: Da Capo Press, 1969 (reprint of 1896 edition).

Military Order of the Loyal Legion of the United States, Massachusetts Commandery. *Civil War Papers.* Vol. 2. Boston: Printed for the Commandery, 1900.

Military Order of the Loyal Legion of the United States, Michigan Commandery. *War Papers.* Vol. 2. Detroit: James H. Stone & Co., 1898.

Newhall, Frederic, *With General Sheridan in Lee's Last Campaign.* Philadelphia: J. B. Lippincott & Co., 1866.

Nichols, George Ward, *The Story of the Great March from the Diary of a Staff Officer.* New York: Harper & Brothers, 1865.

Olcott, Mark, and David Lear, *The Civil War Letters of Lewis Bissell.* Washington, D.C.: The Field School Educational Foundation Press, 1981.

Owen, W. Miller, *In Camp and Battle with the Washington Artillery of New Orleans.* Boston: Ticknor and Co., 1885.

Porter, Horace, *Campaigning with Grant.* New York: The Century Co., 1897.

Prowell, George R., *History of the Eighty-Seventh Regiment, Pennsylvania Volunteers.* York, Pa.: Press of the York Daily, 1901.

Rhodes, Elisha Hunt, *All for the Union: A History of the 2nd Rhode Island Volunteer Infantry.* Ed. by Robert Hunt Rhodes. Lincoln, R.I.: Andrew Mowbray, 1985.

Rodick, Burleigh Cushing, *Appomattox: The Last Campaign.* New York: Philosophical Library, 1965.

Sherman, William T., *Memoirs of General William T. Sher-*

man. Westport, Conn.: Greenwood Press, 1972.

Simms, William Gilmore, *Sack and Destruction of the City of Columbia, S.C.* Ed. by A. S. Salley. Freeport, N.Y.: Books for Libraries Press, 1971.

Sorrel, G. Moxley, *Recollections of a Confederate Staff Officer.* Dayton: Morningside Bookshop, 1978 (reprint of 1905 edition).

Stern, Philip Van Doren, *An End to Valor: The Last Days of the Civil War.* Boston: Houghton Mifflin Co., 1958.

Stiles, Robert, *Four Years under Marse Robert.* Dayton: Morningside Bookshop, 1977 (reprint of 1903 edition).

Stowits, Geo. H., *History of the One Hundredth Regiment of New York State Volunteers.* Buffalo: Matthews & Warren, 1870.

Taylor, Emerson Gifford, *Gouverneur Kemble Warren: The Life and Letters of an American Soldier, 1830-1882.* Boston: Houghton Mifflin Co., 1932.

Tremain, Henry Edwin, *Sailors' Creek to Appomattox Court House, 7th, 8th, 9th April, 1865.* Ed. by J. Watts de Peyster. New York: Charles H. Ludwig, 1885.

United States Department of the Interior, National Park Service, *Appomattox Court House National Historical Park, Virginia.* Handbook 109. Washington, D.C.: GPO, 1980.

United States War Department, *War of the Rebellion: A Compilation of the Official Records of the Union and Confederate Armies.* Series 1:
Vol. 46, Parts 1-3. Washington, D.C.: GPO, 1894.

Vol. 47, Part 2. Washington, D.C.: GPO, 1895.

Upson, Theodore F., *With Sherman to the Sea.* Ed. by Oscar Osburn Winther. Bloomington: Indiana University Press, 1958.

Wainwright, Charles S., *A Diary of Battle: The Personal Journals of Colonel Charles S. Wainwright 1861-1865.* Ed. by Allan Nevins. New York: Harcourt, Brace & World, 1962.

Wildes, T. F., *Record of the One Hundred and Sixteenth Regiment: Ohio Infantry Volunteers in the War of the Rebellion.* Sandusky, Ohio: I. F. Mack & Bro., 1884.

Wilson, William L., *A Borderland Confederate.* Ed. by Festus P. Summers. Pittsburgh: University of Pittsburgh Press, 1962.

Wise, George, *History of the Seventeenth Virginia Infantry, C.S.A.* Arlington, Va.: R. W. Beatty, 1969 (reprint of 1870 edition).

Wise, John Sergeant, *The End of an Era.* Ed. by Curtis Carroll Davis. New York: Thomas Yoseloff, 1965.

Yearns, W. Buck and John G. Barrett, eds., *North Carolina Civil War Documentary.* Chapel Hill: The University of North Carolina Press, 1980.

Other Sources
Bradwell, I. G., "Fort Steadman and Subsequent Events." *Confederate Veteran,* Vol. 23, 1915.

Civil War Times Illustrated. Special Appomattox Campaign Edition, April 1975.

Cullen, Joseph P., "The Siege of Petersburg!" *Civil War Times Illustrated,* August 1970.

Day, William A., "The Attack on Fort Stedman." Unpublished ms.

Funkhauser, Robert D., "Fort Steadman — 'So Near and Yet So Far.'" *Confederate Veteran,* Vol. 19, 1911.

"An Incident of General Keifer's War Record." *The National Tribune,* April 29, 1882.

Johns, B. T., "Sailor's Creek." *The National Tribune,* April 28, 1887.

Jones, A. C., "Third Arkansas Regiment at Appomattox." *Confederate Veteran,* Vol. 23, 1915.

Katz, D. Mark, "Gen. Gibbon and the Captured Confederate Battle Flags." *Incidents of the War,* fall 1986.

Kurtz, Henry I., "Five Forks — The South's Waterloo." *Civil War Times Illustrated,* October 1964.

McClintock, D. R., "Fort Steadman." *The National Tribune,* September 24, 1885.

Moffett, W. W., "Capt. Joseph M. Anderson." *Confederate Veteran,* Vol. 20, 1912.

Robinson, F. C., "Sailor's Creek: The Capture of General Ewell and His Corps." *The National Tribune,* August 18, 1887.

Stewart, William H., "The Hardships of Hatcher's Run." *Confederate Veteran,* Vol. 19, 1911.

Timberlake, W. L., "The Retreat from Richmond in 1865." *Confederate Veteran,* Vol. 22, 1914.

PICTURE CREDITS

Credits from left to right are separated by semicolons, from top to bottom by dashes.

Cover: Painting by Richard Norris Brooke, West Point Museum Collections, U.S. Military Academy, photographed by Henry Groskinsky. 2, 3: Map by Peter McGinn. 8, 9: Library of Congress. 10, 11: Courtesy The Historical Society of Berks County; Library of Congress — The Western Reserve Historical Society, Cleveland, Ohio; Library of Congress. 12, 13: Library of Congress. 14, 15: Library of Congress (2) — State Historical Society of Wisconsin. 17: Confederate Museum, Charleston, S.C., photographed by Thomas P. Grimball III. 18: Library of Congress. 19: Courtesy Bill Burner; courtesy Erick Davis Collection. 21: Painting by Julian Scott, courtesy The Kennedy Galleries, Inc., New York, photographed by Henry Groskinsky. 22: Library of Congress. 23: Library of Congress; U.S. Army Engineer Museum, Fort Belvoir, Va., photographed by Michael Latil — The New-York Historical Society. 24: Courtesy Chris Nelson. 26: Courtesy Frank & Marie-T. Wood Print Collections, Alexandria, Va. 27: Courtesy Bill Turner. 28, 29: Courtesy Historical Society of Delaware; National Archives Neg. No. 111-B-2517 — from a sketch by A. W. Warren, courtesy Frank & Marie-T. Wood Print Collections, Alexandria, Va. 30: Courtesy John T. Spach. 31: Michigan Department of State, State Archives. 32, 33: Library of Congress (2) — from a sketch by A. W. Warren, courtesy Frank & Marie-T. Wood Print Collections, Alexandria, Va. 35: Map by William L. Hezlep. 36: Museum of the Confederacy, Richmond, Virginia. 37: Courtesy Frank & Marie-T. Wood Print Collections, Alexandria, Va. 38, 39: Painting by Sidney King, National Park Service, Petersburg National Battlefield, photographed by Katherine Wetzel, inset courtesy Harry Roach, *Military Images Magazine.* 40: Courtesy Greg Coco, copied and photographed by A. Pierce Bounds. 42, 43: Library of Congress; top right, Massachusetts Commandery of the Military Order of the Loyal Legion of the United States and the U.S. Army Military History Institute (MASS-MOLLUS/USAMHI), copied by A. Pierce Bounds — map by William L. Hezlep. 44, 45: National Archives Neg. No. 111-B-398; Library of Congress — Special Collections (Orlando Poe Collection), U.S. Military Academy Library, West Point, New York, photographed by Henry Groskinsky; National Archives Neg. No. 111-B-368. 46, 47: Library of Congress; inset courtesy Joseph P. Laico, M. D. Collection, copied by Greg Schaler. 48, 49: Library of Congress, except top right National Archives Neg. No. 111-B-5241. 50, 51: MASS-MOLLUS/USAMHI, copied by A. Pierce Bounds; Library of Congress. 53: South Carolina Confederate Relic Room and Museum, Columbia, photographed by Bud Shealy. 54: National Archives Neg. No. 111-B-4282. 56: Drawing by Theodore Russell Davis, courtesy Museum of Fine Arts, Boston, M. and M. Karolik Collection of American Water Colors and Drawings, 1800-1875. 57: Inset courtesy *Civil War Times Illustrated* — drawing by William Waud, Library of Congress. 59: From *The Story of the Great March,* by George Ward Nichols, published by Harper & Brothers, New York, 1865. 60: Courtesy Frank & Marie-T. Wood Print Collections, Alexandria, Va.; South Carolina Confederate Relic Room and Museum, Columbia, photographed by Bud Shealy. 61: South Carolina Confederate Relic Room and Museum, Columbia, photographed by Bud Shealy. 62, 63: South Caroliniana Library, copied by Charles E. Gay. 64: Drawing by Thomas Nast, courtesy Museum of Fine Arts, Boston, M. and M. Karolik Collection of American Water Colors and Drawings, 1800-1875. 66: Library of Congress. 67: Courtesy Georgia Department of Archives and History. 68: Valentine Museum, Richmond — Kean Archives, Philadelphia. 70: Drawing by Karl Jauslin, courtesy The Kennedy Galleries, Inc., New York, photographed by Henry Groskinsky. 71: L. M. Strayer Collection, copied by Brian Blauser. 72: Official Record Map, courtesy Frank & Marie-T. Wood Print Collections, Alexandria, Va. 73: Valentine Museum, Richmond. 74: From a sketch by James E. Taylor, courtesy Frank & Marie-T. Wood Print Collections, Alexandria, Va. 75: North Carolina Museum of History, Raleigh, photographed by Steve Muir. 77: Painting by George Peter Alexander Healy, The White House Collection. 79: Pennsylvania Capitol Preservation Committee. 80: Painting by James E. Taylor, courtesy The Kennedy Galleries, Inc., New York, photographed by Henry Groskinsky. 83: Map by Walter W. Roberts. 84: From a painting by A. G. Redwood, Library of Congress. 86: Courtesy Bill Turner, except bottom right Museum of the Confederacy, Richmond. 89: Library of Congress. 91: Painting by Alfred Chartran, West Point Museum Collections, U.S. Military Academy, photographed by Henry Groskinsky. 93: Map by William L. Hezlep. 94, 95: Civil War Library and Museum, Philadelphia, copied by Brian C. Pohanka — courtesy Frank & Marie-T. Wood Print Collections, Alexandria, Va. 96: Drawing by Alfred R. Waud, Library of Congress. 97: Courtesy Bill Turner. 98: Painting by William L. Sheppard, Virginia Historical Society, Richmond — Museum of the Confederacy, Richmond, photographed by Katherine Wetzel (3). 100, 101: Library of Congress. 103: Special Collections (Orlando Poe Collection), U.S. Military Academy Library, West Point, New York, copied by Henry Groskinsky. 104-107: Library of Congress. 109: Courtesy Chris Calkins, photographed by Katherine Wetzel. 111: MASS-MOLLUS/USAMHI, copied by A. Pierce Bounds; courtesy William Gladstone Collection. 113: Courtesy Rufus Barringer, photographed by Gus Johnson. 114, 115: Map by William L. Hezlep. 116: From a drawing by Alfred R. Waud, courtesy Cooper-Hewitt Museum, Smithsonian Institution/Art Resource, New York. 118: Courtesy The Rhode Island Historical Society. 119: Map by William L. Hezlep.

121: Courtesy William Gladstone Collection; Mrs. E. B. Custer Collection, Custer Battlefield Museum, Crow Agency, Mont. 122: U.S. Army Engineer Museum, Fort Belvoir, Va., copied by Michael Latil. 123: Virginia State Library, Richmond. 124: From a painting by Gilbert Gaul, from *Battles and Leaders of the Civil War*, Vol. 4, published by The Century Co., New York, 1887. 125: Painting by William D. Washington, Virginia Military Institute, Preston Library, Lexington. 126: Valentine Museum, Richmond — from *Battles and Leaders of the Civil War*, Vol. 4, published by The Century Co., New York, 1887. 127: Courtesy Lon W. Keim, M.D., copied by Jimmy Krantz. 128, 129: Painting by William Trego, West Point Museum Collections, U.S. Military Academy, photographed by Henry Groskinsky. 130: Courtesy Chris Nelson, photographed by Michael Latil; MASS-MOLLUS/ USAMHI, copied by A. Pierce Bounds. 132: Library of Congress. 135: Courtesy Chris Calkins, photographed by Katherine Wetzel. 136: From a drawing by William L. Sheppard from *Battles and Leaders of the Civil War*, Vol. 4, published by The Century Co., New York, 1887. 137: National Archives Neg. No. 111-B-2735. 138: Map by William L. Hezlep. 139: From a painting by William L. Sheppard, from *Lee and Longstreet at High Tide: Gettysburg in the Light of the Official Records*, by Helen D. Longstreet, published privately, Gainesville, Ga., 1905. 141: Courtesy Chris Calkins, copied by Larry Sherer; from the original by R. F. Zogbaum, from *Harper's New Monthly Magazine*, April 1898. 142, 143: Drawing by Alfred R. Waud, Library of Congress. 146: Painting by Thomas Nast, Galena-Jo Daviess County History Museum, photographed by James Quick; painting by Louis D. Guillaume, Appomattox Court House, photographed by Ronald H. Jennings — painting by Tom Lovell, © 1969, National Geographic Society. 148: From a drawing by William L. Sheppard, from *Battles and Leaders of the Civil War*, Vol. 4, published by The Century Co., New York, 1887. 150: Drawing by Alfred R. Waud, Library of Congress. 151: Courtesy Cal Packard, photographed by Robert A. Grove. 152: National Archives Neg. No. 111-B-4358; Maine State Archives, Augusta — drawing by J. R. Chapin, Library of Congress. 154, 155: Courtesy D. Mark Katz. 156, 158: Library of Congress. 159: Sketch by Edward W. Kemble, Print and Picture Department, Free Library of Philadelphia, photographed by Arthur Soll. 161: Map by William L. Hezlep; Library of Congress. 162: National Park Service, Fort Sumter National Monument. 164-171: Library of Congress.

INDEX

Numerals in italics indicate an illustration of the subject mentioned.

Time-Life Books Inc. offers a wide range of fine recordings, including a *Rock 'n' Roll Era* series. For subscription information, call 1-800-621-7026 or write Time-Life Music, P.O. Box C-32068, Richmond, Virginia 23261-2068.